Soul Sister Letters

Compiled by Anita Sechesky

Soul Sister Letters – Let's Talk About Love, Faith, Abundance & Divine Purpose
Compiled by Anita Sechesky

Copyright © 2020 LWL PUBLISHING HOUSE
A Division of Anita Sechesky – Living Without Limitations Inc.

All rights reserved. No part of this publication may be reproduced, distributed or transmitted in any form or by any means, including photocopying, recording, or other electronic or mechanical methods without prior written permission of the publisher, except in the case of brief quotations embodied in critical reviews and certain other noncommercial uses permitted by copyright law. For permission requests, write to the publisher, addressed "Attention: Permissions Coordinator," at the address below.

Publisher's Note: This book is a collection of personal experiences written at the discretion of each co-author. LWL PUBLISHING HOUSE uses American English spelling as its standard. Each co-author's word usage and sentence structure have remained unaltered as much as possible to retain the authenticity of each chapter.

LWL PUBLISHING HOUSE
Email: lwlclienthelp@gmail.com
Website: www.lwlpublishinghouse.com

Book Layout © 2020 LWL PUBLISHING HOUSE

Soul Sister Letters – Let's Talk About Love, Faith, Abundance & Divine Purpose

Anita Sechesky – Living Without Limitations Inc.
ISBN 978-1-988867-52-6

Book Cover Design: N. Sechesky
Inside Layout: LWL PUBLISHING HOUSE Editorial Team

Table of Contents

Legal Disclaimer 1

Dedication 3

Foreword 5

Meet The Visionary 9

Acknowledgments 11

Introduction 15

Section One

Chapter One - Anita Sechesky 23
  DEAR SISTERS OF THE WORLD

Chapter Two - Anita Sechesky 27
  SHINE AND SHOW UP LIKE A DIAMOND

Chapter Three - Anita Sechesky 35
  SELF LOVE

Chapter Four - Anita Sechesky 41
  LOVE FOR THE INNER CIRCLE

Chapter Five - Anita Sechesky 45
  LOVE FOR THE GREATER GOOD

Section Two

Part 1 - Love & Friendship

Chapter Six - Rose Marie Young 51
    SOUL SISTER LETTER

Chapter Seven - Koreen Bennett 55
    SOUL SISTER LETTER

Chapter Eight - Dominique Dunn Malloy 61
    SOUL SISTER LETTER

Chapter Nine - Anita Sechesky 67
    SOUL SISTER LETTER

Part 2 - Abundance Mindset

Chapter Ten - Rose Marie Young 77
    SOUL SISTER LETTER

Chapter Eleven - Koreen Bennett 85
    SOUL SISTER LETTER

Chapter Twelve - Dominique Dunn Malloy 91
    SOUL SISTER LETTER

Chapter Thirteen - Anita Sechesky 95
    SOUL SISTER LETTER

Part 3 - Divine Purpose

Chapter Fourteen - Rose Marie Young 103
    SOUL SISTER LETTER

Chapter Fifteen - Koreen Bennett 111
    SOUL SISTER LETTER

Chapter Sixteen - Dominique Dunn Malloy 115
    SOUL SISTER LETTER

Chapter Seventeen - Anita Sechesky 121
    SOUL SISTER LETTER

Part 4 - Self-Love & Development

Chapter Eighteen - Rose Marie Young 127
    SOUL SISTER LETTER

Chapter Nineteen - Koreen Bennett 135
    SOUL SISTER LETTER

Chapter Twenty - Dominique Dunn Malloy 139
    SOUL SISTER LETTER

Chapter Twenty-One - Anita Sechesky 143
    SOUL SISTER LETTER

Part 5 - Faith Walk

Chapter Twenty-Two - Rose Marie Young 151
    SOUL SISTER LETTER

Chapter Twenty-Three - Koreen Bennett 159
    SOUL SISTER LETTER

Chapter Twenty-Four - Dominique Dunn Malloy 163
    SOUL SISTER LETTER

Chapter Twenty-Five - Anita Sechesky 167
    SOUL SISTER LETTER

Section Three

Chapter Twenty-Six - Anita Sechesky 175
    NO GREATER LOVE

Chapter Twenty-Seven - Anita Sechesky 181
    LOVE...IT'S WHAT YOU'RE WAITING FOR

Chapter Twenty-Eight - Anita Sechesky 187
    SHINING LIKE THE DIAMOND I AM

Chapter Twenty-Nine - Anita Sechesky 193
    LIFE'S INSPIRATIONAL MILESTONES

Chapter Thirty - Anita Sechesky 197
    GOD'S LOVE IS MY HOPE

Conclusion 207

Co-Author Portfolio 211

Your Legacy Story 219

Legal Disclaimer

Soul Sister Letters - Let's Talk About Love, Faith, Abundance & Divine Purpose does not substitute any form of professional counsel such as a Psychologist, Physician, Life Coach, or Counselor. The contents and information provided does not constitute professional or legal advice in any way, shape, or form.

All chapters are written at the discretion of and with the full accountability of each author. Anita Sechesky - Living Without Limitations Inc. or **LWL PUBLISHING HOUSE** is not liable or responsible for any of the specific details, descriptions of people, places or things, personal interpretations, stories and experiences contained within. The Publisher is not liable for any misrepresentations, false or unknown statements, actions, or judgments made by each author in this book, who is responsible for their own material and has shared their information in good faith to encourage others.

Any decisions you make and the outcomes thereof are entirely your own doing. Under no circumstances can you hold the main author (Anita Sechesky) **LWL PUBLISHING HOUSE,** or Anita Sechesky - Living Without Limitations Inc. liable for any actions that you take.

You agree not to hold the author, **LWL PUBLISHING HOUSE,** or Anita Sechesky - Living Without Limitations Inc. liable for any loss or expense incurred by you, as a result of materials, advice, coaching or mentoring offered within.

The information offered in this book is intended to be general information with respect to general life issues. Information is offered in good faith; however, you are under no obligation to use this information.

Nothing contained in this book shall be considered legal, financial, or actuarial advice.

The main author (Anita Sechesky) or Publisher assume no liability or responsibility to actual events or stories contained within.

The advice contained herein is not meant to replace the Professional role of a Certified Professional Coach, pastor, minister, physician, or any medical advice. Please consult with a doctor or family physician.

Anita Sechesky and/or **LWL PUBLISHING HOUSE** do not guarantee to make any of our clients or readers Best-Selling authors. This status is a result of combined efforts through professional coaching and self-motivation.

Dedication

This book is dedicated to all the special women friendships in my life, especially my beautiful mom, who is my role model and hero, for all the loving wisdom and courage she has blessed me with.

I'm so thankful for all the women in my life and ask God's blessings over you always.

I also honor all Godly, sister friendships around the world.

May you continue to bloom where you are planted and release all brokeness from your past.

Thank you everyone for being who you are. God's perfect love made no mistake when He created you.

Love, Your Sis

Anita Sechesky

Foreword

Women come in a variety of shapes, colors, and sizes. Our beautiful and voluptuous, yet strong and resilient features are uniquely different. We come from diverse places and life experiences. Everything about each one of us is a priceless masterpiece that God himself formed within our mothers' wombs. It is those intricate differences that make us exactly who we are. A masterpiece is defined as anything done with masterly skill. A masterpiece is valuable and handled with great care. There is a tenacity and attention to bringing out the beauty and value in that individual masterpiece, thereby increasing the value through attention to detail.

I have seen this laser attention to detail in my relationship with Anita Sechesky, who is the powerhouse visionary behind this insightful compilation featuring three other Soul Sisters whose hearts are dedicated to living a divine purpose. Anita has a deep desire to help you see the beauty that is unique to you. When you meet her and engage with her, she sincerely wants YOU to realize this truth for yourself. So, it is with this intention she seeks to help us acknowledge the beauty we as women have been blessed with. In her brand-new book *Soul Sister Letters - Let's Talk About Love, Faith, Abundance & Divine Purpose*, this award-winning author uses her God-given gift of brilliant writing along with her amazing co-authors to highlight aspects of their life journeys and how love at the core has been essential to who they are becoming. They pull back the curtain of their hearts and souls and give us a peek into their real day-to-day lives. We are reminded of the love of God that is foundational to all of our breakthroughs. We are relational beings and it is through our interactions that we come alongside each other to become the best that we were designed to be. Created in His image, we understand and appreciate the love that God has for us and this changes the way we show up in life. Do you understand and have you really embraced the fact that He loves the YOU and all that makes YOU beautiful? God, your Creator, loves you not based on your wardrobe choices, hair, fashion, or the size of your accomplishments. Simply put, you are loved just as you are.

Friendships are extremely important and while we hear so often about women tearing down, competing, and comparing, there is hope. Remembering our identity in Christ and understanding who we are in Him, we behave differently. It's worth repeating – you are loved! You are priceless! It's a new day. We are beginning to embrace strong female friendships again.

The Soul Sister authors believe that God's love is a bond or glue that foster's strong female bonds. As we build each other up, we are inadvertently building ourselves as well. We can encourage and empower each other because we are not competitors, but we actually complement one another perfectly. As we do this from an Abundance Mindset, we become supporters of each other's dreams and aspirations. Our Faith Walk deeply encourages our personal growth in Christ. When we cheer each other on, we form a community of strong believers and can courageously hold each other accountable to be faithful and grow in knowledge and love. Therefore, we are all better for it.

That's why I believe that for every season of our lives, God blesses us with exactly what we need, whether it's that loving and strong female friend to support us on our journey or we become that light of hope and healing for another. This book belongs on every household shelf to reach for time and time again when you're feeling overwhelmed by life's burdens and need to come back to who you are as a sister in Christ.

Remember, no one is an island! Soul Sister, we cannot build that beautiful community without being in a community.

So, join me. Grab a coffee, let's read some letters, and talk about God's love for us all.

Pastor Pat Russell

Reverend Patricia Russell is a Certified Leadership Coach, Certified Prepare Enrich Facilitator, Speaker, Premarital/Marriage Counselor, Worship Leader, Author, Soloist, and Songwriter. Her gifts have been shared internationally with audiences of all ages to encourage, empower, and share life lessons in word and song. Patricia has served in ministry for over twenty years and was a regularly scheduled soloist on *"Living Truth,"* a program that aired from the People's Church in Toronto, Canada. She's also had the honor of being the guest soloist on Living Truth's inaugural tour to Israel. Patricia has recorded two gospel/inspirational CD's *"Lord I Trust You"* and a live recording of *"Draw Me Nearer."* She has authored a booklet titled *Lord I Trust You - Words of Encouragement* and is the Visionary Compiler of *Stronger Resilience - 30 Stories to Empower the Mind, Body & Spirit*, set to be released in 2020 through **LWL PUBLISHING HOUSE**. Patricia is happily married for thirty years and has two adult children.

Email: patrussellsings@gmail.com

Instagram/Twitter @patrussellsings

Facebook: Patricia Russell Music and Speaking

Meet The Visionary

Anita started her successful Canadian business, **LWL PUBLISHING HOUSE**, seven years ago because she felt unappreciated and insignificant growing up. Therefore, she wants her authors to feel empowered and validated when they write their stories working with her. If people don't write their life legacies when they are physically, mentally, and spiritually capable, they won't feel like they've honoured what they've walked through. As a result of publishing a genre of self-healing publications based on faith, hope, courage, healing, success, and positive mind set in an array of beautiful publications, emotional and spiritual healing through forgiveness when writing has been her primary focus when working closely with her clients.

Anita believes in supporting individuals from all walks of life to step into their next level of accomplishment. As a Registered Nurse with over twenty years in Health Care, she has worked with all age groups and diversities, Anita is also the immediate Past President of the Brampton Chapter of the Holistic Chamber of Commerce.

She is a highly skilled Registered Nurse whose professional role encompasses the Charge Nurse and Team Leadership position in a variety of healthcare settings from Nursing homes and hospital floors with specialized areas such as the Cardiac Procedures. As a Trauma Nurse, she has worked in the ED of various hospitals throughout Southwestern Ontario.

She has been recognized as one of the Top Ten award-winning Women of Inspiration in the GTA, nominated under the Author's category in the prestigeous Waterfront Awards, Holistic Book writing mentor branding 460+ Canadian and International Best-selling authors in the last seven years. Not only is she the Founder of Anita Sechesky - Living Without Limitations Inc. but she's also the Owner and Publisher of LWL PUBLISHING HOUSE, the 2nd division of her main company which empowers, inspires, and motivates both authors and their readers alike to step into living their best lives possible.

To Living Your Blessed Life,

Anita Sechesky

RN, ICF-CPC, Founder, CEO & Publisher at LWL PUBLISHING HOUSE,

#1 & Multiple Best-Selling Author, Holistic Book Writing Coach, Ghost Writer, Keynote Speaker, Workshop Facilitator, Conference Host, INSPIRED TO WRITE Podcast Host

Email: lwlclienthelp@gmail.com

Website: www.lwlpublishinghouse.com

Facebook Business Page: LWL PUBLISHING HOUSE

Facebook Business Page: Living Without Limitations in Print

Facebook Private Group: 2020 INSPIRED ACTION - PLAN TO SUCCEED!

YouTube: Anita Sechesky - Living Without Limitations Inc.

Spreaker: INSPIRED TO WRITE Podcast

Acknowledgments

A special thanks of love and gratitude to God, my Heavenly Savior, for placing this vision in my heart. I admit it has been simmering within me for years, but God knew the timing to bring it forth and with His approval, I am blessed to present it with my wonderful Sisters in Christ.

I give thanks to my parents for all the love, dedication, and support they have each blessed me with. Even as an adult, I stand corrected many times over and for that, I am grateful to have such wise and thoughtful parents to help me when I cannot see things as they are.

Mom, I thank you for being my best friend and best Sister friend in Christ. You have shown me the example of what it means to be a woman of God from the time I was a young child. I have seen your courage and willingness to hear God's voice and obey. You are my inspiration and I pray that God will continue to bless you with good health, peace, strength, longevity, wholeness, and happiness all the days of your life. I pray that you will live to see your grandchildren have children and so many more bountiful blessings. Amen.

Dad, I thank you for being an example of a Godly Father, provider, protector, and wise counsel to me and my brother growing up and now to my children. I am so blessed to have a dad who dedicates his life to meditating on God's word daily. I have seen the strength of your faith and admire the peace that is within you. Your example is a blessing to your family and all those who know you. I pray that God will bless you with good health, peace, wholeness, strength, longevity, and happiness all the days of your life. I also pray that you will live to see your grandchildren have children of their own and that you receive so many more blessings. May God's light always shine upon you. Amen.

To my Husband Stephen; Thank you so much for all the support and dedication you have given me over the years and especially to help this book come to life. You are such a blessing to me and our family as well as our clients. I pray God's blessings of peace, health, wholeness, joy, and abundance over you in every area of your life. May God's hands always be upon you. I ask God to bless and protect you always so we will live a long life together seeing our children's children grown and so many more blessings. Amen.

To my sons Nathaniel and Sammy; Thank you both so much for being the blessings you are to me as I have worked in putting this publication together. I pray God will bless the works of your hands and that everything you touch will prosper. I ask God to also protect you in all your ways and that you will always hear his voice. As you grow, may you see God's hands in everything you do. I pray that your lives are richly blessed and God will show you the plans he has for your life; to prosper and not harm you. I also pray that you will have the discernment of God to know what is real and what is a trap of the enemy. May God's angels continue to guide and protect you both as you live a long and prosperous life. Amen.

To my brother Trevor; I want to thank you for being a blessing in my life. Thank you for always encouraging me to pursue my dreams and believing in me. I am blessed to have you as my brother. I pray for your protection that you will always hold God close to your heart and that when he speaks you will hear him. I also pray that God will grant you all the desires of your heart as you seek him diligently in all your ways. Amen.

To Rev. Patricia Russell; Thank you so much for writing such a poignant and powerful foreword to emphasize the purpose of God's girls in relationships. As the body of Christ, we need to establish healing among ourselves and not push the undesirable situations under the carpets because they will affect the body as a whole; the end result possibly leading to sisters and their families leaving churches and the faith altogether. Your message is powerful, and you are a blessing to me. I pray God continues to use you for His Glory in all your ways. Amen.

To my Co-authors;

Rose Marie Young – Thank you so much for your unwavering friendship. You have shown me what a sister relationship is all about by standing by me from the time we truly connected by sharing our hearts in conversation. You are a blessing and I'm so excited about how your Sister letters will now be a blessing to all those who read them. This is just the beginning of your journey and I'm blessed to share this moment with you. I pray God's blessing of love, abundance, and blessings over you all the days of your life. Amen.

Koreen Bennett – Thank you so much, Sis, for being who you are. From the time I met you and the countless tea meetings in my living room, it has been unquestionable that you were a friend who is committed to prayer and relationship. I'm grateful to have you in my life and pray that as you grow through your healing, you will come out even stronger. God is not finished with you yet, dearest Sis, and I know the best is yet to come for you. I pray God's blessing over you as you walk in his anointing. Amen.

Dominque Dunn Malloy – Thank you so much for allowing yourself to become vulnerable so you can help others be empowered, heal, and grow spiritually. It's been a pleasure working with you and I look forward to more opportunities in the future. I know that God is not finished with you. I pray that you will hear God's voice, guidance, and direction as He wants to prosper and bless you in so many ways. Amen.

Introduction

This book was powerfully inspired by the Holy Spirit and individual life experiences that each one of my co-authors and I have walked through to be where we are today. As Christian women, we all agreed it's difficult at times to navigate our way through situations when the world expects us to react and respond differently. However, at the same time we, as children of the Most High God, must be mindful of the way we conduct ourselves and remember that we are not permitted to treat God's children like rubbish and expect God to hear our prayers as we try to worship Him and pursue His blessings.

I presented this beautiful vision to my co-authors specifically because I felt led to do so. I did not dig into their life experiences and determine if they were "qualified" in any way, shape, or form. In fact, I truly believe it was because we are all different that God inspired me to approach them when I did for this project. The only thing we most definitely have in common, without a question of doubt, is our rock-solid faith. I knew this was exactly what was needed to get what was required to make this book come together. We are all different ages and we have not known each other for a long time. It is only within the last few years that we have connected and felt the indescribable bond that makes us sisters in Christ. One is a newlywed in her early adulthood, just starting out her married life together with her husband; another is a single mother of three adult children and a grandma to three beautiful grandchildren; the third one, who recently endured the excruciating pain of losing her eldest child, is a married mother of a wonderful preteen son as well as being the loving grandma to her departed son's child; and finally there's me: a wife and mother of 2 wonderful sons and 2 fuzzy fur babies.

You will find this book to be very unique as you'll discover perspectives that will be great for a ladies group discussion or Christian book club. It will help you to question things in your own life and challenge yourself to step into a better position of power as a child of the Most High God. We all share how life has helped us to grow into the people we are today. As the Compiler of this compilation, I was seeking to help our readers find connections among the females in their own lives by understanding that many of our thoughts, dreams, and life experiences, although vast, can be a starting point to find the friendships we all desire for ourselves. It's not a greedy thing to want a good friend. King David and Jonathan were the best of friends; Ruth and Naomi were of different ages, yet they were there for each other; Jesus had twelve sworn friends who committed themselves to become part of his tribe (the terminology we use today). I believe on a grand scale, our Christian sisters are a unique group throughout the world. We hurt deeply because we feel deeply. We are easily persuaded to open our hearts, forgive, and trust over and over again. We are the nurturers and life providers as we birth our children. We are healers as we help to mend wounds, emotions, and lives with our gentleness, kindness, and generosity. We are the homemakers who can make something simple feel like the most luxurious of things to our family and friends. And we are the entrepreneurs who work from our homes to offer financial stability and care for those under our protection, guidance, and love. Maybe it's because of a lack of teaching or teaching that does not actually apply to the average Christian woman and her many challenges or vulnerabilities that we can actually become a target for the enemy of our soul to continually hurt us. For many, we take it personally not fully comprehending that we haven't actually done wrong to cause so much pain and disappoints in our lives.

I want to also recognize the countless women in our family of God who, sadly, have been hurt by the leadership, or individuals, within their own church communities. This is a far more serious thing in my opinion than many care to address. I personally fit into that same category and will go so far as to say I have often been misjudged because of my ambitions and eagerness to do more for God. I have actually found in my experiences that there are discrepancies in the body of Christ that is often overlooked. Jealousy has no place as does competition. We all know that many are called to serve God in ministerial positions, but we must also remember that few are chosen. You might have a passion to speak or evangelize. Seek God and ask Him to guide you to your divine helpers who will help to make the way to your position in Christ. There will be a time when we all stand before God and according to the Gospel of Matthew, *"Not everyone who says to me, 'Lord, Lord,' will enter the kingdom of heaven, but only the one who does the will of my Father who is in heaven. 22 Many will say to me on that day, 'Lord, Lord, did we not prophesy in your name and in your name drive out demons and in your name perform many miracles?' 23 Then I will tell them plainly, 'I never knew you. Away from me, you evildoers!"* Matthew 7:21-23 (NIV). Basically, it's the love in our hearts towards others that God is truly looking at, not title, not positions, not qualifications, not money, not accomplishments or even who we are connected to. It's always been about Love. Without love, we can speak, yell, and stand on any platform with a million people in attendance, but if we hold one thing against a sister or brother in Christ or a sinner not saved as yet from grace, we are nothing in the sight of God.

I pray that as you read the following pages within this book, you will be stirred up according to His purpose. You will be encouraged, inspired, healed, find restoration, and even repent if you feel the Spirit of God moving in your life. God is not finished with you, dear Sis. He's only just begun!

Sinner's Prayer for our Sisters:

Dear Jesus. I humbly come before You and ask You to be the Savior in my life. I seek Your forgiveness for all the things I have done wrong. Please help me to be the woman that You need me to be. Restore my broken pieces so that I can feel Your loving peace and receive Your salvation all the days of my life. Amen. (John 3:16)

You are not the limitations that people place on you. You are exactly who you choose to become.

—Anita Sechesky

Section One

Chapter One

DEAR SISTERS OF THE WORLD
by Anita Sechesky

If you knew how amazing you are, you would never allow another person to ever hurt you again. You must know the people who belittle and cause destruction in the souls of others are bitter and broken with no love and compassion for themselves. As we show mercy and empathy for those around us, our hearts have a greater purpose to bring healing for everyone. The way people project their emotions is quite often a reflection of what's happening within them. Life is not always how we expect it to be and there are days you may feel like throwing in the towel. It's in those moments that I encourage you to step back and reflect on how far you've already come. Sure, there may still be a long way to go to achieve your goals. But your journey has always shown you the depth of your dreams, even though you still can't see the bigger picture as it beautifully, and yes sometimes painfully, unfolds before you. You will always find your strength within if you seek a higher power such as God, the Creator, and Heavenly Father. It's amazing what a simple prayer cried out in times of struggle and surrender can do for your broken spirit and lost soul in a world of hate, contempt, and jealousy.

I implore you to never be hard on yourselves and don't take out your frustrations on the very people who care so deeply for you.

They are hurting just as you are when things don't work out as you anticipated. The loved ones we have close to us are the people who feel the deepest desire to see us succeed. Give them a little more compassion and patience for they are not purposely driven by the passion and God source you may be following. In fact, they just believe in you, just as you are. They don't ask questions, instead they just willingly give of themselves to help bring your dreams to life.

It's not always easy to love someone with a deep commitment for something bigger than self, just like it's not always easy to understand why others are jealous, spiteful, and lacking appreciation and acceptance of who we are.

You will find that life presents you with so many opportunities to connect with multitudes of individuals, but please have wisdom and guard your precious and beating heart. It's in the very moments of inspiring others at their starting points in life that you may stir up something ugly in someone who will never appreciate the knowledge, encouragement, and inspiration you freely pour into them. You see, it's already inside of them Their own ugliness becomes mixed with the jealousy that grows as they witness you striving and jumping over hoops and high towers – you suddenly became a target for competition. They will try to use your naivety and kindness to reap as much information from you. And when things are exposed into your spirit of who exactly they are, they will conveniently lose you to someone else that's up and coming or eagerly looking for someone to follow. Like attracts like, so this is a good thing when you lose those so-called "friends" because they never really were friends. In fact, I would refer to individuals like that as "fiends who suck out the positive energy from you." They glean as much as they can before exiting your life as painfully as possible. Don't let them get that chance to hurt you. Know who they are now and release! Release! Release! Then start focusing on all the love that surrounds you. You are loved and appreciated by so many; why be discouraged any longer by the few who were never meant to be a part of your life. We each evolve and are still growing into our true authentic and loving self. It's your time to continue your journey without any limitations of negativity.

There will come a time when you will see "flashing lights" around certain people I have just described, but unfortunately not until a few have made their way onto your path so you can learn to identify their selfish and false personalities immediately. I have learned quite quickly that when people tell you they were divinely sent to build you up or take you to that next level, it's time to arm all your security systems on the Homefront. From my own experience, they always show up loud and leave loud and proud. Sadly, they will never achieve what they are after because of their lack of wisdom and integrity. This shortcoming will always hold them back until they make things right and release their own personal past identities in exchange for a clean and clear conscience.

For you my dear sisters of the world, you should know you have the right and freedom to own your emotions, strengths, and creativity. Allow yourselves to be divinely guided and never permit something to block your perception of how to live a life without limitations. You dreamed it and now it's time to achieve it!

Love Your Life,

Anita Sechesky

Excerpted from *Shine Like a Diamond - Compelling Stories of Life's Victories*

You are creating the world around you by the beauty in your words.

−Anita Sechesky

SHINE AND SHOW UP LIKE A DIAMOND
by Anita Sechesky

When I think of an empowered woman, I think of all women around the world, the wives, mothers, grandmothers, aunts, cousins, and sisters. Not of a particular race, religion, or orientation. Nor do I imagine one body type: short, tall, slim, medium or heavyset, dark or light-colored skin, straight or curly hair. For me, I look at the essence of what being a woman really is, which is the combination of her mind, body, and spirit. This is what truly makes a person who they are, not skin color, language, education, heritage, or social status.

From the time I was a young child growing up in a small isolated Northwestern Ontario community (a far cry from my luscious and tropical birthplace of Georgetown, Guyana), I have searched both inside my heart and soul, and outside in the environment I was growing up in, to find out who I really am. What am I supposed to look like? What should I wear? How do I present myself? My journey has led to hurtful places of rejection amongst people I thought would accept me because I am, after all, a "female" just like them, but unfortunately, many people want to identify with their "own kind" no matter how far we may go in becoming a society based on equality for all. This has been the ongoing dilemma I have observed on social media and in the world. I see this very attitude continue in so many ways and innocently provoking the very nature of the human spirit to stand up for what they believe is right or what they feel they deserve. I have nothing against improving one's life and the quality of how you live your life, but it is rather disturbing when I see any kind of division and calling together of the individual races to stand up, show up, and speak up. I don't believe in the harshness – there is a time to be bold in one's journey and there is a time to be appreciative of what has been already historically achieved. To think differently is creating a negative mindset where there should be none.

For me, regardless of who is doing it, it brings back many memories of feeling left out and lonely in a world I was subjected to this Canadian environment based on the best interests of my parents. When nothing is said about these negative and accepted events taking place, people will silently and naively continue the self-segregation by passing on the attitudes of low self-esteem, and negativity to the next generation, sadly disregarding what has already accomplished through peace and war so many years ago by lives that are not being respected for their sacrifices to make this world a better place for all.

I guess what I'm trying to say is please reconsider those events which only nominate and celebrate a certain type of people. Don't let your whole world revolve around these types of events because what will eventually happen is your perspective will become so narrow-minded, you will slowly forget that all people matter, all life comes from a woman's womb regardless of what nationality she is, what language she speaks, the color of her skin, her hair type, etc.

All human blood is the same color and regardless of the blood types, each ethnic race has every different blood type as well, so we are already equal underneath our skin. It's up to us to see this and make our attitudes reflect that of human unity and acceptance of all. The woman is a special gift to all. She is the source of life and without her, there is no life to sustain the human race. We are all one and the same. Acceptance begins within each one of us. Go ahead and celebrate your cultural differences and uniqueness – it is what makes you who you beautifully are. But please don't become so absorbed that you forget we all need each other on this planet to live in unity – after all, there is only one race – the human race!

This leads me to "Why" I compiled this long-awaited book, which is very dear to me because it covers so many facets of a woman's heart. For me, it has been within my spirit for longer than I can remember to write about why it is so heart-wrenching to be a woman. You see, women are very hard on each other and because we oftentimes are so fixed in our mindsets and behaviors, we are difficult to convince otherwise. What I really mean to say is that we take each other for granted and expect more than we should even though we would never consider ourselves to be accountable for the same level of expectation. We always think we can do better and if some other woman is rocking her stuff, we have a deep desire to either compete with her or be jealous because we didn't do it first. When we should be building each other up, we look for the pettiest of things to point our fingers at and suddenly that woman is the worst "b*****" there ever was. We cut off relationships like we change our undergarments and we spitefully use and speak badly of other women because we don't like something about them or maybe we don't think they deserve what they've achieved or gained in life. We take credit for something that is not ours to own, yet we would never like it if someone did the same towards us because we always think we are so much better than them. We say we forgive, but we keep talking down about our sisters until we have stomped them into the ground. We make promises we don't keep and get mad when others let us down. How could they? We assume things so easily about other women, yet we have no clue what they are living through, walking through, and enduring on their journey. As women, we do and don't live like sisters. When we have faith, we are the first to doubt and steer the whole crowd wrong, yet we never humble ourselves and walk in meekness. As women of strength, we are the first to lose our words of encouragement when we see other women needing support to go through their own labor pains to victory. As women of honor, we are the first to lose our integrity by gossiping, back-biting and putting others down. I have experienced all of this in some way or another in my life whether it was in my own family or among peers and even clients. Women are mean!

So why do women deserve to be encouraged to "Shine Like a Diamond" and celebrate for being a woman? It's certainly not for all these negative, damaging, and destructive traits that each one of us as women possess. You might be the nicest person on the block, but I'm sure there is some other woman out there that would sadly say otherwise about you. God bless you, sweetheart. I have learned in my own life journey that people will always project what they are on you. You may never hurt a single insect, but someone will say otherwise of you. People don't always want to know the truth which would set them free from their own limited mindsets, instead, they prefer to be content with something they are familiar with. That is why I went to great lengths to describe so many personality traits and behaviors above. They are merely descriptive words that represent an identity that is either true or false. It is up to us individually to determine which of these representations truly reflect who we are and how we show up in the world as women filled with integrity, courage, and faith who are emotionally balanced in body, mind, and spirit.

Trust me, I've had my own emotionally weak moments in my hairdresser's chair feeling like I should start my own group and empower "my own kind." After all, it's what everyone else is doing! Then I quickly come back to reality and realize had my beautiful daughter Jasmine Rose lived to see what I was contemplating at that very moment, it would break her heart. You see, my children are both Guyanese, mixed with an East Indian heritage, and Caucasian mixed with Canadian, English, and Polish descent. With so much world travel and international business and trade over these past decades, the rise of inter-racial marriages has risen significantly and will continue as mixed children marry other mixed children creating even more beautiful "global" babies. This brings me back to my very question "Why are there so many ethnic groups promoting 'All _____' events and no one is saying anything?" If it was organized and promoted as an "All white" event, there would be so much chaos and confusion. Please don't allow yourself to be caught up in the Spirit of Division, because it really is a spirit that takes hold of a person's mindset, bringing in their friends called hate, jealousy, and animosity and all their other friends. Just like the saying goes, "Show me who your friends are and I will show you exactly what you are."

This book was beautifully created from the heartstrings of each one of my contributors, who decided they wanted to be part of something bigger than themselves.

The stories and inspirations in this book are aligned to the vision that God placed into my heart at a very young age. I knew what it felt like to be the one who didn't fit in. I was different in my physical appearance as my family immigrated to Canada from Guyana, South America when I was just a young child at the sweet age of four. My skin tone reflected the beautiful golden hue of being born a warm, lush, and tropical country. There, I had already been introduced into the Nursery School system with great friends. I was accepted and loved for who I was. I remember going out when it rained tropical buckets – there were huge mud puddles to jump in afterward. My once playful and carefree life was instantly transformed as we relocated to Northwestern Ontario, Canada. I had to learn a whole new way of adapting into a society that was in the middle of a winter deep freeze with temperatures ranging from minus 25 to minus 40 below. Yes, it was a very brutal cultural shock for all of us. Not only was the climate cold, we soon discovered that the citizens in that part of the world were not the warmest at times either.

So you see, my vision of resilience to overcome all limitations that life throws my way has always been a part of who I am as a person. When I grew up, I trained to become a Registered Nurse who cares for all people regardless of race, color, religion (creed), gender, age, national origin, or disability. There is no discrimination in health care just as there shouldn't be in all the other areas of our lives.

I learned tolerance at an early age. My life training involved understanding that a huge part of acceptance towards others encompassed searching my own heart to understand that people are always going to respond based on how they are feeling and what their personal experiences are. Who am I to judge? My parents are my heroes in every sense of the word. They have taught me to accept people who would never accept me and to forgive others who would never forgive me. You see, life is all about choices. Love and peace are unlimited because they come from God, whose profound peace is unlimited towards us. The more love you give, the more you get back. It may not come from where you imagine but it always does come back to find you and lift you up when you least expect.

Every one of the passages within this book comes from viewpoints that are quite incredible when you really begin to understand that each person encounters challenges, yet despite different experiences, we feel similar emotions on the journey of discovering who we are. This validates that we're all connected some way by our energies and ultimately in a spiritual sense. I encourage you to search deeply within your hearts and souls, permitting yourself to safely expose your emotions so that you can discover any unhealed areas in your life today. As you find more Hope, Love, and Peace along with Faith, I trust that you will appreciate the energies connected to the words and emotions from your past negative experiences in comparison to what you want in the future. It always surprises me how the human spirit is so strong and resilient to endure the things we face but not always brave enough to talk about without possibly feeling shame, embarrassment, or fear of ridicule.

Personally, my faith and positive mindset brought me through so many unpleasant and often times despairingly awful experiences in life, although I admit it was the love and awareness that I have very precious people who appreciate me for who I am. I never take that lightly as my own parents were both raised with only one parent figure in their lives at a young age, and they still became the best parents they could be for my brother and I, despite their lack of full parental influence. Many times, people do not realize that the reason they are struggling is due to the love and peace missing somewhere in their emotional make-up, whether it is from a parent, child, spouse, relative, or friend. Choosing to live a life filled with Hope is what connects all of our positive interactions in the bigger picture.

For those who are still lacking courage in your lives or you cannot find a way to heal the emptiness, and have become so discouraged, my message for you is to never give up! You are like that Diamond in the rough – your life experiences are making you stronger and helping you to come out shining brighter. What you seek will always find you. You will come across people in this life who will only point out your weaknesses or mistakes as they see it. Don't react, instead accept it. You are beautifully created and perfect, but you are evolving each and every day, so you're allowed to be imperfectly perfect. It's what gives you the human edge and it's what makes you better the next time around. Let people judge you and project themselves in your evolution. It's the best they can do and it's their weak and insecure way of trying to hold you back in life. It never works if you let it all go and keep moving in the direction of your dreams. Forgive those who have damaged your perspectives and dreams. You can still appreciate that there is a world of like-minded individuals waiting to embrace you in warmth and acceptance. Hope is what the world needs, and just like a priceless Diamond never loses in value, you are only getting better and better. Keep grinding through and allow your Creator to refine you in the beautiful light of love where you will shine even brighter!

Excerpted from *Shine Like a Diamond - Compelling Stories of Life's Victories*

SELF LOVE
by Anita Sechesky

In order for an individual to acquire a true nature of love for self from a heart of gratitude, there must be a divine connection to source, whatever you may perceive that to be. We all come from somewhere outside of who we are in our physical state of being. For some people, this means there is the belief of a divine connection to the Creator of our universe. Ultimately, we must appreciate that all lives are intricately fashioned in such a way for us to continually evolve into our greatest self. We, in turn, must fearlessly journey within our hearts and souls to discover the secret passion that will propel us into well-being and bliss. It's not an easy journey as many will admit. We are our own worst critics and many times the limitations and perceptions that we hold onto are based upon the most perplexing or difficult experiences and unfortunately, we still tend to embrace labels that were attached to us during those times of vulnerability and negative life events.

As creatures of habit and reaction, we base a majority of our life's journey on things that we are comfortable with regardless of the damage it is causing us. Many times, we stay within our comfort zone of awareness, refusing to step outside the box or take a chance on what possibilities may come. In doing so, we remain stagnated in our emotional, mental, and even spiritual growth, all the while physically progressing. As we continue to age and develop, our physical identity and appearance changes, our behaviors are second nature, and our choices have become predictable to those around us.

In order for there to be real growth and evolution, we must choose or allow new and thought-provoking experiences to challenge our very core. You see, sometimes stagnation is misinterpreted for peaceful tranquility and oftentimes peaceful tranquility is misconstrued as bliss. When an individual testifies to reaching the ultimate awareness of inner peace and harmony, magnified by the power of love and contentment, they are very well describing the state of bliss. This is the oneness with your environment and everything within your soul. It's up to you to determine where life is taking you on your path of personal evolution. As you experience more challenges, satisfactions, imperfect relationships, and mental stimulation through advanced training and skills, or just by reading this book, life will always test you to change your reactions and predictabilities. The choice is always yours, just as your emotional response attached to it.

Many who come to a place of serenity have chosen to enter into a space of sacred gratitude and appreciation of life. They come into the understanding that in order to co-exist in a world of so much misrepresentation, corruption, and negativity, one must be able to understand the center where their heart and soul is at complete peace. This may be achieved through a connection to God or the universe – something much bigger than any of us. This space will have to be where there's an abundance of peace and love. Speaking from a heart of grace and acceptance, you must be able to control or manage situations and circumstances which you may never have been able to do before.

For someone to achieve this state of gratitude, they must understand that life is a story that they get to co-create. Our thoughts create our reality, based on our emotional attachment to the outcome. People often equate miracles and optimistic results to the understanding that they have deposited a measure of faith, good thoughts, and positive affirmations towards their generated outcome. Many times, life's harsh experiences are the contributing factors causing people to demand within themselves that which makes them invincible. Past events have established a foundation of strength and tolerance, enabling individuals to be empowered so that they won't just endure any more setbacks, but instead, choose a to live a life that responds to the joyful nature of having stillness and not mindlessly reacting as they may have done in the past.

Along life's journey, the human spirit perseveres through many trials, tribulations, and triumphs. As we are tested from many directions, we develop a template of our personalities. The compositions throughout this book touch on things of the very nature of personal endurance, hope and strength. For instance, developing and seeking a life of gratitude can begin in childhood based on both negative and positive events. It will impact the very essence of that person who experiences those situations to seek out, question, challenge, and change past, present, and future events. These may include: not fitting in, not understanding what love looks like, having to face life-threatening conditions, an unexpected pregnancy, abusive relationships, family breakdowns or dysfunctionalities, as well as a variety of other reasons. What happens may not be directly connected to who you are, but life will give you many experiences related to the vibrational energy of those you are closely associated with or what you are presently experiencing. You may just happen to be a recipient from the spillover of those you have interacted with. People do not realize that each and every relationship in their lives is part of a profound and intricate network of the many facets and roles they have to support as individuals. It doesn't have anything to do with whether they are negative or positive, the very fact that you are connected with others is a confirmation that you exist. How often do you actually take time out to appreciate all that you have around you, whether it is close and loving relationships, friends, or families? Even the individuals who have opposed you have played a critical role in developing the appreciation of the real and pure gift of love that you have in your life. Hate will never measure up to love. Love's power dispels animosity in every way possible because love is at the very core of being a compassionate and caring human being. As a mother loves her child, so is the pure love that each human being possesses. Love is what we are all created from and we are all positively receptive to receiving it wholeheartedly and without conditions as it is in the very will of survival.

Are you grateful for what you have endured? In order to be recognized and appreciated, you must be validated. That means you have a personality, an opinion of how you perceive life, and how you choose to show up in the world. By understanding that your life has equal value, just like the people you are connected with, allows your higher self to appreciate and connect with others on a more authentic and sincere level. This is very significant for those who been emotionally scarred from neglect, abuse, or traumatic experiences. Although this may have happened unexpectedly, it DOES not mean it was the victim's fault in any way, shape, or form. It just means that now the awareness of the distressful circumstances has actually strengthened the individual enough for them to shift from a victim mentality to one of self-empowerment where they are capable of seeking the solutions to improve their own perspectives and chose how their past experiences will define them.

That being said, you enter into self-development and transformation modes and become an enlightened being who recognizes and appreciates the greatness that is within you and how magnificent a gift it really is to rediscover what you have lost through your journey. Suddenly, you're facing your own situations and relationships, careers, and opportunities from a self-love perspective. Now it's all about you and how you're managing your life. No one else is accountable but you. In doing so, you are forced to make decisions all over again, as you get to choose love for self despite what you have already walked through.

A heart of gratitude is cultivated from such profound and often times life-altering experiences. A familiar saying states that people will continue doing the same thing over and over, expecting a different result each time. Unfortunately, they don't recognize that the key solution is introducing a whole new perception that opens windows of possibilities, allowing room to breathe and grow. I often wonder about how it would impact the lives of those who seem to be stuck in a difficult and lonely state if they would only choose to be open-minded enough to appreciate that in order to love the life they have been blessed with, they must develop a continual process of forgiveness and love in their lives. Releasing the baggage and heartache resulting from the unforgiveness and pain of others, as well as themselves, will allow the trapped negative energy and low vibrations to be changed. As they choose to make an effort of forgiveness and gratitude in their thought processes, verbal responses, emotional triggers, and behavioral reactions, it will bring positive and higher vibrational energy that the power of love is comprised of. This change of attitude will continue attracting more of the same positive experiences and it will feel like a huge weight has been lifted off.

For anyone to gain a life of blessings and bliss, one would have to choose to be loved and accept everything that has ever happened to them as they cannot change the past, but can only create a future of happiness, peace, and love. It may take a whole journey revisiting and finding strength in the journey, or it may take a simple contemplation of accepting life as is and moving on – no looking back. Forgive and forget.

I will be honest – from my own experiences, unresolved events in life will always result in some stagnation and blockage of blessings.

I prefer to choose wisely and forgive. My health, well-being, and happiness are worth so much more than holding onto something from the past. Life is always how we chose to make it and a whole renewal of perspectives can powerfully create major shifts in positive future outlooks and outcomes.

Love for oneself from a heart of gratitude is one of the most gratifying journeys you can enter into. May your travels be enlightened and full of love.

Excerpted from *#Love - A New Generation of Hope Continues...*

LOVE FOR THE INNER CIRCLE
by Anita Sechesky

As we explore the area of love for others, it's imperative to be fully aware that in order to have a relationship with another human being, one must be willing to open up their heart and allow vulnerability to their emotional connection, which allows others to become an extension of who you truly are. Often times our perceptions of people, whether they are relatives, friends, colleagues, or other interest groups, represent an exterior facet of our deepest desire to belong and be connected. We either accept it or not. We categorize ourselves according to emotional attachments. Yes, there are times that although we are related to different types of individuals, we aren't truly connected. In fact, we are just playing a role of association as there may be negative emotions from past experiences that affect these relationships from being established on a deeper and more intimate level.

That being said, when we are aware that we cannot change anyone but ourselves, our true evolution of awareness and enlightenment naturally begins. Suddenly we can see how valuable the connections we have in life really are. As this awareness becomes relevant, our discovery and appreciation that we are all on a journey is significant in every sense of the word. For instance, we are now tolerant of things that were beyond our scope of understanding. There may have even been times we didn't value our relationships for what they were and how they presented themselves in our self-centered lives. Personal relationships validate our very being and do not judge or disregard our best interests. They just simply acknowledge the very fact that we exist and are appreciated for who we are. These relationships have the ability to continually empower and educate us as we step into the path of our greatest selves ever. How amazing is that?

It's because of these personal connections, we are confident to carry on. They surround us like a cushion of comfort in a world that is harsh and cold. Everyone wants to belong, but what does it take to develop these deep emotional soul ties that will be our strength when we are weak, our compass when we are lost, and our affection when we are rejected in the world? You see, many successful people started somewhere when no one knew who they were, and they probably experienced anxiety, stress, or discouragement. Yet, at the very moment, they were going to let it all go, someone close to them gave them that pat on the shoulder, made that cup of tea, or gave them that inspirational talk. These are the common roles that parents, siblings, spouses, children, mentors, or true friends do best. The world does not know or care about you as these people do. They have already invested their time, lack of sleep, finances, dedication, and energy to pour into your dreams and desires just as you more than likely have done for them. This IS the difference between inner circle relationships compared with everyone else. You don't need to beg or pay them for their loyalty and support. They will be your greatest fans and although they may let you down at times, don't take offense. They are only human like you and I. Anyone who can tolerate us in our worst possible state of mind, you can be certain will stick around and help you to get through moments of fear, failure, or negativity.

For me personally, my inner circle relationships were pivotal in my self-development process which has always been an ongoing facet of who I am because of how I choose to show up in the world. Whether it was my family, spouse, children, or close friends, I highly regarded their opinions and perspectives even though I may not have always agreed. By allowing myself not to become easily offended by others, I took the time to evaluate and examine the process of offense by others in my life. Choosing to operate from a mindset of possibilities and unlimited potential strengthened my inner circle relationships. The value that arose enabled me to greatly appreciate how others who were close to me actually cared so deeply for my well-being. You will always be surrounded by people unless you live on an isolated island. Everyone has their own lives and activities to keep them busy and involved. However, the individuals that are close to you will need you just as much as you need them. This will empower your progress as your attributes evolve and define you as an individual.

When was the last time you stopped and thought back to when you were growing up, and how your family interactions brought joy and a sense of belonging? Maybe there was a family joke, related to past memories, that kept going or maybe there was a love so deep that it brought you through the worst possible experience. These are the bonds that strengthen and grow deeper as the years go on. Nothing can replace this kind of comfort when no compassion can be given. Because we are spiritual beings, we are connected on such a deep level. This is referred to as unconditional love because there is no definitive explanation of what it may consist of. It just means that the relationship between two people, not necessarily romantic, but on the same plane of existence strengthens and supports one another. You can always depend on these people to come through for you. Just as a parent loves their child, so can a true friend love you as you are.

I encourage you to seriously examine all your relationships within your inner circle. As a Registered Nurse, I have personally observed how traumatic it is when family members lose their loved ones, especially when there are gaps in the communication process and the emotional, spiritual, and physical bond of visiting and being present are broken. Many times, I have seen precious souls leave this world with broken hearts and spirits because of family disputes and disagreements. It's a sad thing to see the look in their eyes, worried if their loved ones will come to see them before their departure. Our lives have no guarantees, but we can make the choices to love and place value where it belongs. Once life is over, there are no second chances as we know of. Love is all there is and all there ever will be when all else is gone.

Excerpted from *#Love - A New Generation of Hope Continues...*

Chapter Five

LOVE FOR THE GREATER GOOD
by Anita Sechesky

When was the last time you actually realized you were someone else's outer circle relationship? You had no emotional connections to this person, yet there they were doing something to help make your day or life better. Maybe you had gone through something serious or traumatic requiring assistance, or it could have been as simple as having car troubles and that one person was the only one there to help you out. You didn't refuse their assistance and it was thoroughly appreciated with love and gratitude because they saved you a whole lot of stress that day.

My reason for including this as the third theme within this beautiful anthology is that I realize we can never address love and gratitude for others enough in our lives. We are all connected and with that awareness, we can come to a greater appreciation of others. Personally, I believe that this is exactly what the whole concept of world peace is all about – reaching out to help others who may never be able to ever reciprocate it. We all have a role in how we choose to make a difference in the lives of those around us who are not part of our everyday interactions.

Normally, we just go about our daily lives not considering what's going on outside of our immediate outreach. Social media has made it seem that the world is in our backyard. When we hear the latest news of what's happening somewhere else, we either react and respond right away or we tune out of that particular event, as it may overwhelm us outside of our comfort zone or our physical reach. In reality, nothing can be further from the truth. Although we see via our computers, smartphones, television, newspaper, or hear on the airwaves, we are still connected in a dysfunctional sort of way. We are triggered to evoke emotional responses based on the fact that we are compassionate beings with extensive personal outreach. We share life experiences and memories with so many major or minor role players. This explains why, when we hear of disconcerting things like natural disasters and disease outbreaks, we become concerned because of the fear of vulnerability and of how it may affect so many lives. As a result, there are many people who choose to step outside of their familiar settings and risk their health and well-being or sacrifice their time to help make a difference in the lives of complete strangers. When a person begins to understand how valuable their small acts of kindness and generosity are for the greater good, and how the impact becomes immeasurable and so much more valuable, it becomes a heart-warming experience.

Each contributor in the next section all share a common goal or vision – engaging their lives in some way to help those outside of their close inner circle. They can see the greatness in all people and believe that everyone deserves a chance to create a better life for themselves. It is truly an honor to partner with people of such high caliber and integrity.

I believe we all contribute to the greater good, at times consciously unaware of it, by supporting, for example, a local organization that in turn sponsors an international humanitarian project. I'm sure that if we carefully examined our connections in life, we would find so many individuals that dedicate themselves in some way to help make a difference in the world. I also believe that one must truly love themselves and those close to themselves in order to purely love others outside their immediate circle without hesitation. How could they honestly love those with whom they have no biological connection? The true reality in loving yourself requires you to let go of everything that does not serve your greatest self any longer. Choosing to love your inner circle connections or those who know and appreciate you sets your love apart. If you don't allow others to negatively influence you, you'll always attract love back into your life. You have made your love factor very focused and clear. You are Love! In a sense, this increases the value that you see in yourself because you choose to not allow others to control your thoughts and opinions about your love for others.

When you consider the time it takes to manage our responsibilities and roles, think how much more of an added accountability it is for others to do so with a free mind and will. I believe it takes a person with a big heart to appreciate the life they have, all the relationships they've been blessed with, and even extend themselves to people who will never say "Thank you" or try to repay the kindness and generosity they have received.

This world is filled with people who possess so much potential, yet feel their lives are insignificant. They no longer have dreams or desires because they are discouraged and demoralized by life. This confirms why I believe there is so much remaining for us to do, whether in the smallest to the greatest of ways that we see possible. If we choose to help others, who are hopeless and without passion, make a better life for themselves and their loved ones, then we have brought a little piece of heaven to earth. There are already many established organizations worldwide that can use the support, and then there are things we can do right here in our neighborhoods: food drives for homeless shelters, assisting on community organizations, winter coat collection, harvest cupboards and distribution. Many churches, volunteer, and community services always need support. The point is for us to get started if we have never done so before.

I have volunteered with fundraisers to help build financial assistance so that a particular organization can assist families who have lost their homes in fires, sent shoeboxes filled with toys and personal care items to countries for needy children, and supported local and international health care charities. Many organizations participate not only locally, but with international relief. Choose yours wisely and if applicable, choose one that's closest to your heart.

I know that our world is filled with beautiful people. I have provided nursing care to people from various regions around the world. My experience has always been very positive, and I appreciate everyone equally. One thing that consistently stands out is that language is never an obstacle when it comes to matters of compassion and care. What an amazing world full of precious souls we have. Let's help to bring love to every corner of the globe and apply liberally with empathy and grace.

Excerpted from *#Love - A New Generation of Hope Continues...*

Section Two

Part 1

Love & Friendship

*Life is more
precious
when you
see your
humanity
reflected
in everyone.*

~Anita Sechesky

SOUL SISTER LETTER
by Rose Marie Young

Dear Sis; I know sometimes you may feel like a child looking out into the world and everything may seem enormous through your beautiful eyes, but nothing is as it seems to be. I encourage you, my dear sweet sister, to first find love within yourself so that the cold, harsh world will not destroy the innocence within your soul. Life is not always easy, but if you have a good sense of who you are, you'll be strong enough to overcome anything that comes within your path. You will find your way as you grow and love yourself even more.

I know it won't be easy, but you're ambitious and smart enough to understand how to get through as you mature each day into the beautiful person God intended for you to be. Know that you are stronger than you think. You are an incredibly beautiful soul, that's who you are. No matter how old or young you are, the world will often see you as small, but by knowing yourself, you will always stand tall.

Friends may come and friends may go. Just know that you should always be number one in your heart; love yourself no matter what. Not all friends will be true; remember that some will chase your heart and some will break it too. These are times that you should also know that not all friends are meant to stay, and some will even lead you astray. It's when you lose a "so-called friend" that you will grow stronger, wiser, and you will understand life is sometimes that way. When this happens, it will hurt. Your heart will break but just know when we lose people not meant for us, we open our hearts to better people who will help us grow into a more virtuous version of ourselves. At times you may feel abandoned, unhappy, or even unloved. You may even feel like harming yourself, but don't you dare harm a single hair on your head.

You are strong. You are smart and you can overcome anything. If you ever feel alone, you have a God that is bigger than life itself. With Him, you are never alone. So, don't be afraid to face challenges because you have a God that will guide you through. The world is a big and scary place, but He will give you the strength and courage to get by and as you grow through these tough times, it will make your path an easier one. You, my dear child, are a gift to this world. Just know that without your presence, so many lives will not be the same.

My dear Soul Sister, its such a beautiful day and I am writing this letter to shed some light on the love and relationships that may come your way. You have always had questions that were left unanswered even to this day, and I know you are very wise. Even though you don't frequently get the answers you seek, you have always wanted to know the "what," the "hows," the "wheres," and the "whys." My letter to you today is about love and friendship. It will help you prepare for the amazing woman you will one day become. Although it may seem a long way off, your future is not too far from now. When it comes to yourself, Soul Sister, I know that you will surely fall in love. I can not give you the details about who you will love or when because the future is not for us to see.

Although you may be all grown up now or you may still be very young, I want you to know there is so much more to learn about true love and friendship. Love is definitely not about kisses and hugs. It's not even about the gifts that you get for Christmas It's not about the sweet candies, teddy bears, and flowers on Valentine's day. It is not about the cake and presents you received on your birthday. Love is respecting yourself and others, and it's about you loving yourself as a precious gift from God. Yes, your parents and your family may or may not love you, but as you grow you will learn that each relationship you build when you are young may seem innocent and fun, but never forget to love yourself first. Love and friendship are both important and as you grow, you will see that not everyone you love is meant to be a part of your life. Not everyone in your present is meant to be a part of your future. My dear Soul Sister, I'm telling you this because you need to understand that sometimes you don't know when these relationships are going to start or even when they're going to end. But don't be afraid. Just trust yourself. Not all relationships are the same. Some may feel like a game and that's very unfortunate, especially when you call someone your friend and trust them. Some will be true as they respect you with great admiration, while others will utilize your love and friendship for their own purpose. In that case, you need to know, my dear Sister, that those so-called friends are just using you. Always remember to protect your heart. The word love can be misleading. I suggest you question all of the motives of the ones that say they love you and get clarification from the start. I'm not saying that you won't get your heart broken at some point because sometimes people are not who they say they are.

My advice is to align yourself with people who have similar interests and values as you do. Contact with people who believe in you and respect you and your feelings. These are the people that will have your back and hold your hand when things go wrong.

My dear Soul Sister, as you grow more and more each day into the beautiful woman that you were meant to be, remember to put God first in your life. He will help you make good choices and build relationships that are healthy. Always let Him lead and guide you.

Some friends may influence you to do things against His will and lead you astray. So be wise when you are choosing your friends. Each relationship will affect you, and sometimes your friends will represent you in your absence when you're not able to defend yourself.

My dear Soul Sister, I know with all the life experiences that you've been through, God was always there to help you each step of the way, so don't be afraid to love. He will always be there beside you. Love freely, always stay true to yourself, and never forgot that you, my dear Sister, are an example and an expression of God's true love.

You are the leading lady in your life. Give yourself all the attention that you deserve. You are wonderful and you are kind. You are courageous and brave. Although you have been through so many ups and downs, you have never given up your will to climb nor your will to survive. I know it was because of God's good grace that you found your strength to reach inside your soul and become motivated and inspired to love yourself. You are a leading lady. Learn how to fight without violence. You have shifted your mindset and have chosen to treat yourself with an abundance of love. You, my dear sister, are that leading lady of your beautiful and abundant life.

Rose Marie Young

You can read Rose's next letter on page 77.

SOUL SISTER LETTER
by Koreen Bennett

Dear Sis; I'm going to say my first experiences, but significant relationships began at childhood growing up as the elder sister of four younger siblings. I would love to share about how nice it was being the older sister because my sisters looked up to me as their mentor and role model. I was their teacher, caregiver, music teacher, and dance choreographer. During many talks (later in life), I was told I was their motivator and the person they would come to when they needed help for anything in life. For example, I was there to teach them how to coordinate their outfits. I would help with their hairstyles, applying lip gloss/make up, making beds properly, and advising them on almost everything, basically like a second mom. Because I was depended on so much, I honestly didn't realize that I had to grow up ahead of my age until I was in high school where I felt free enough to experience real relationships with others outside of my family circle of responsibility. It was in these teenage years that I truly appreciated that I could be valued differently and not just needed. I finally learned that real relationships were really about allowing myself to be a girly girl and not think about any other responsibilities. Don't get me wrong, I love my sisters. Our relationships were great, although we still had fights – you know, as all girls do. But we were always able to come back together in spite of our differences and love each other as if it didn't even happen. We couldn't stay mad at one another because that was part of our deep sister bond. This is why I would say that those early years of my life showed me that friendship and growing together are strengthened when we form a really deep connection of trust. I always said that when you have such a connection with someone, all the ugly fights and arguments are just that; but this is where the real test of friendship is and began.

My first two friendships outside my sibling relationships were with two special individuals from different ethnic backgrounds. The first one was in grade school and the second one was in middle school. In both of these friendships, we became quite close like sisters to one another. We used to share lunches, sat beside each other in classes, shared secrets, and it was like we were inseparable once we were together at school. Sadly, my grade school friend and I only lasted in those short, sweet years because we were going to different schools. My second best friend (BFF) was an awesome friendship with another sister of a different race and we connected so strongly, it was as if we had known each other forever. We could talk about anything and everything for hours and hours, again mostly about boys and make-up. It was so much fun to find someone who was like my equal. She understood and accepted everything about me. I remember getting a gift for my fourteenth birthday from my friend: a teddy bear that I still have today because of that special friendship. I don't know what it was. We just really connected but I'll never forget how that relationship showed me I was not only important and valued, but cherished.

Another experience (more teenage experiences) I had that I'll never forget was in that same year. One morning, I finally got my period just before going to school. I was freaking out of course because there I was; eight o'clock in the morning, class starting at nine o'clock, and guess who shows up? I didn't want to go to school, so I went to my mom where we had a good talk and then she provided me with the mattress of doom, aka, the maxi pad. So, I had no choice but to go to school that morning. I was so embarrassed and uncomfortable but still excited because I got to tell all my girlfriends that I was finally a part of the club. I was no longer a girl but now a woman. Those girls already had their periods, so I was the last of the bunch. They all hugged me and congratulated me. Actually, it was like a big **PERIOD** Party. Crazy, right?

Well, middle school was cool and all, but again, friendships were shortened as everyone went their separate ways for high school. Losing really great friendships were difficult. I'll never forget those two girls despite our short relationships. However, I was blessed once again to find another amazing friend in high school. Hey, she was my first African Canadian friend. Of course, we hit it off right from the start and even though she was just a little tiny thing, I refer to her as my little Guyanese firecracker because we were the complete opposite. While I was comfortable behind the scene, she was the one who constantly pulled me out to experience life with a little more excitement. I was always more the shy type of girl while she was very strong-willed, confident, and she knew what she wanted in life. We complimented each other very well. For example, while I was still trying to figure out who I was as a young girl and teenager, she reminded me to enjoy my teenage years and live life. We did a lot of things outside of school together and even went to a couple of parties (hopefully my mom won't read this so I have to explain, "ha-ha"). I remember it as if we had a little clique; as if we were sisters. Unfortunately, it was also my first time experiencing a girl break-up where it left unresolved and painful feelings. To this day I'm not sure what happened. I know there was an argument between the two of us, and then we were no longer friends. Sadly, this was also the same time I moved out of my hometown of Toronto. Over the years we never really connected again as there was no social media and easy access to find someone online at that time. I encourage you my sisters; never leave broken relationships alone. Try to bring healing so that there will be peace between you and that other person to move on to other beautiful friendships without any residual energy lingering around you that can harm it.

After that experience, because we never spoke again, it made me sad because we did have a lot of good times together. What I learned from that relationship with her was that we complemented each other even though there were obvious differences. She was bold and confident; I was more reserved and not sure of myself. I felt that she was petite and had a really nice figure and more accepted than me, while I was still trying to figure out my body image and where I fit into the world, something all of us sisters can relate to. I hope that I was not the only one. She showed me that I can be confident in my own skin. Interestingly, with many of the talks and views on life, I took what I thought would be good to share with my own sisters. My friend was like a mentor to me as I was to my sisters. Yes, we were the best of friends, but I also saw her as a Life Coach; someone who taught me a few life lessons.

So, in conclusion, my Sisters, what I want you to take from my letter to you is that you'll go through life and have many sister friendships. Some will be joyful and some will be heart-breaking, but at the end of the day, they would have given you the experiences to hopefully be a better woman. Whether it was a good experience or not-so-good experience, it will shape the girl, the woman, the wife, the mother, the sister, the leader, the coach, and the mentor that you are or will become. I say this to you, my sisters: enjoy your sister friendship relationships. I believe every woman who comes into your life comes there for a reason and/or a season. Some might be there for a moment or for a lifetime. However short or long, enjoy the moment and treasure the experiences.

Can I show some love for our fellas, my Sisters? To the special guy in our lives, we appreciate your friendship, your love, your patience, and how you try to understand the way our minds work. There are some fellows out there who have given us sisters a listening ear, a shoulder to lean on, and some comforting words. I thank you for your support and friendship. I say thank you to my honey who some days, NO!!, most days does get on my last nerve (love you babe), but I wouldn't trade him in for anything. We tend to not give our men the recognition sometimes, so I say, "Hats off to my Man." Thank You. Love you.

Koreen Bennett

You can read Koreen's next letter on page 85.

SOUL SISTER LETTER
by Dominique Dunn Malloy

Dear Sis; As I sit here and write this, I am filled with joy, excitement, and overflow with love for the life I have and the life you are creating right now. First off, I want you to know that if you're reading this, I'm incredibly proud of the woman you are which includes the woman you are becoming. I don't know where this letter finds you today. You may be at a place in life where you are deeply in love pursuing its embrace, you may still feel the butterflies in your stomach as you think of the love of your life, or maybe you're still on the quest for all the love-filled pieces of the puzzle to fall into place. Either way, the one thing I must say is that I love you, dear Sister, and I'm glad that you're here today. My hope, as well as my desire for you, is that as we take this journey together, you will see yourself all the better for it. Looking back in the years of adolescence where you may be reading this now, I can remember how I occasionally struggled to create deep connections and wonder if sometimes that may also be the case for you. For me, it was mostly because of the color of my skin that we traveled way too often and because of the crazy big glasses and braces I had that made me feel like an alien. For whatever reason you may not feel like you fit in right now, hold strong – for it's in these times when you feel alone that will raise you to greater heights in the future. The real truth is that you cannot have transformation without first being broken. We all may feel broken at one time or another in our lives but it's through the shattered pieces that light is able to shine the clearest.

I remember feeling broken while in grade school. These were the early years when I had just settled in Winnipeg after moving all over Canada with my mom and sister. Our latest trip from the East Coast happened because we were escaping from our stepdad and the harmful lifestyle he was creating for our family. The first year that I was in Winnipeg, my newly adopted pet dog bit me on the face because I was overly affectionate and had disturbed his sleep; it was the learning curve with this new relationship. Even though I grew up with all kinds of dogs, this experience still never changed my love for them because I was always better at relating to animals than with my peers. I found it challenging to connect and form deeper female friendships where I had to become vulnerable with my thoughts and feelings without being questioned or judged. I felt I was different because of my background, physical appearance, and family dynamics as well the instability of even identifying where my geographical home location actually was for fear of having to justify myself over and over again. It was so exhausting living this way in defense of things that I did not create in my family.

Looking back, I feel I had so much difficulty settling into the first year at my new grade school because of the patch over my injured eye which my new pet had suddenly inflicted me with. The one positive highlight about my pirate patch was when my newest best friend C.S. jokingly nicknamed me "Patchy." Our friendship evolved right after I had moved to Winnipeg because I often wandered to the back of the school during recess where he would be playing soccer. I'd show up waving at him, loaded with snacks, sarcastically making jokes about myself to make him laugh and get his attention because that how we connected in the first place. From that moment on we always enjoyed each other's company and became inseparable. I didn't hang with the other girls in class but rather loved to rough house with all the boys on the field, so he often invited me to their lunch table with his other guy friends. They all treated me like one of the boys, probably because I'd have the best snacks around and we all swapped our munchies during recess. I found that it was always easier to form better, more solid relationships with the opposite sex because I either dressed like them or I looked like them with my hairstyle not being fancy and my attire not being girlish. They also found me easier to relate to because I had seemed to have a very positive mindset no matter what. I was not one to gossip or compete with anyone. I didn't talk badly about other people and I believed that's what made me different than most of the girls in my class. Also, I was not interested in projecting a girly self-image at that age so they could appreciate my easy-going personality which was one of the things the guys loved about me being a tomboy, not to mention my great skills at wrestling. As you can see, I always knew that I had to defend myself from an early age, something that I quickly learned from having to escape from my estranged stepfather. As time grew, I found that in the groups I ended up settling into I would somehow become a target for teasing. Even with C.S., our relationship was based on jokes that soon became hurtful, since I allowed it to go on without speaking up for fear of being alone and losing my new friends. I grew into someone who started to believe some of the things about me that were being said. When I could, I'd rather be left alone. I found great love in the books I read, the poems I wrote, and the things I would paint. It wasn't until I started dating years after that my confidence in speaking up grew and I became truly comfortable in my own skin and with my peers who surrounded me.

Another way I learned to connect with my peers as I grew up was on the topic of faith. My mother always enrolled me in bible camp with S.C. which is something I thoroughly enjoyed. My faith was established by my adoptive mom who always tried to instill within me how to pray and trust in God for all of my needs. Despite everything my mom was living through, it always amazed me how she went back to her faith to cope with life in general. She was my first role model alongside my older biological sister who showed me how to have strength and her loving care showed me how to be resilient and overcome anything that life throws my way. Even though my sister never showed her emotions, I could see her courage, maturity, and desire to protect me even as a young child. As for my relationship with my mom, as time passed our relationship once incredibly close would soon grow sunder because I could not understand the struggles she was facing with her own mindset. It often left me frustrated as to why she couldn't see the bigger picture of life beyond where she was currently at. I had always been positive, even at the youngest age that I can remember. When I was being bullied by my friends, I was grateful that I had people around me who took the time to talk about me. Whether it was good or bad, they were talking about me so that made me happy. I remember always thinking about how each situation could be worse and came up with a ridiculously funny story about how it could be even more devastating. I guess when you're a kid, you're not exposed to life's truest hardships and though I could hear the arguments going on within my house, I'm extremely grateful my mom had always painted a fairly secure and stable picture for me when it came to her faith. She would continually say that faith, hope, and love were all that you would need, but the greatest one could have was love. That's what I held onto when I was faced with an obstacle – I'd think how I could give more love into that situation.

I even found that as an adult in those times of great contemplation, I would be triggered by those same old feelings of fear from childhood. One of my most recent experiences, for example, was my marriage proposal. When my husband had first proposed to me, I was afraid probably because I felt like I was still evolving and healing into my best self and now I was facing a life-changing question that would make me vulnerable once again. This relationship with my boyfriend, who was about to become my fiancé, made me face my own inadequacies and strengths. Learning to put my life in some else's hands was a lot to ask. M.M.'s proposal was a big shock, so it coincidentally turned me back to my faith because even though I was unclear of what the future would hold for us, it reinforced to me that life was about faith and not fear, knowing that two are better than one in any situation, and that I am blessed to have had the journey I did so that it would bring him into my life. So, therefore, I was able to eliminate that fear of the unknown of what life would be like with him in the future. Honestly, when I was getting married, those fears were the last things on my mind because I knew that there was something greater waiting for us.

As a result of having a healthy marriage, despite my parents' rocky relationship, I believe our growing faith is a foundation that anchors and intensifies our bond as husband and wife, which interestingly enough has helped build greater adult female relationships. I no longer feel a fear of being vulnerable. The old ways that I used to think of myself, such as not fitting in as I grew up, or not being valuable enough do not apply to this new mature and stronger me. People find me approachable and light-hearted because I love to learn about others and what makes them tick.

This is how I got the privilege of falling head over heels in love with the greatest friend I could ever have – my husband! Like any relationship, it takes hard work, dedication, and loyalty, but there are just a few things I want to touch on in case you haven't found your other half yet. Everything takes time, patience, and courage. From the day I met M.M., the love of my life, I had always focused on what I could give, not what I could receive. Just like my mom told me, focus on love. Don't get me wrong, I was hesitant at first as you may be too, but never forget: you deserve love. A deep overflowing abundance of love is what you were meant to have, so don't settle for one that gives you less.

Dominique Dunn Malloy

You can read Dominique's next letter on page 91.

Everything in my life is a blessing: the good, the bad & the yucky because I get to choose how it will benefit me.

-Anita Sechesky

SOUL SISTER LETTER
by Anita Sechesky

Dear Sis; Life is not always what it seems like when it comes to Love and Friendship. I really want to help you understand how I feel about the things I have walked through in my own life. You see, I believe that many times we are so caught up in who we are at that moment that we forget to guard our hearts. As a result, I have found that there are so many similarities when it comes to romantic love and friendships that I felt it was time we give ourselves permission to talk about it in context.

With romantic love, we allow ourselves the opportunity to bare our hearts and souls to an individual we do not necessarily know everything about because we want to be loved and cared for by someone who we feel connected with. Therefore, we are not being fully aware of the great risk we are taking yet believe nothing bad will ever happen. This very risk is adventurous and exhilarating at the very least because it comes with a range of new experiences that will help us to feel good about life and who we are. On the flip side, although we cannot predict the future, we will find ourselves in situations where we realize that this person is not for us because they don't hold the same passions, dreams, or are not interested in making things work out for the best. At that moment, we know it's over but sometimes struggle with letting go. Always hoping for the best and downgrading our feelings, we believe we're the problem or the reason things are not going well. Eventually, the truth does come out and we stop the madness.

Yes, we mentally and physically let go, but emotionally we still hold on to so many issues about the memories of what didn't work because, as females, we tend to overplay and analyze things in our heads instead of releasing what didn't serve our highest good. All of this goes back to our conditioning as young girls and how we learned that we needed to be proper girls and not tomboys. We had to behave and dress a certain way. I'm not sure if anything is actually wrong with this concept, however, what concerns me as a Christian and Certified Professional Coach, as well as health care provider, is the missing information in between, such as it's okay to be exactly as you are but know that you are also fearfully and wonderfully made in the image of Christ. If God says you are perfect, then believe it! You are perfect.

Jesus had twelve disciples or friends, and even He experienced deception when Judas turned against him. Jesus loved His friends; He shared His adult life's journey with them day by day. They traveled together, did ministry together, and ate together. They were in each other's faces 24/7! They spoke into each other's lives... in fact, they were so committed to serving Jesus they left the lives they were living to join His vision! So, tell me what does your tribe look like? What are they giving up so they can join forces with your bigger picture vision? Are they truly supporting you or are they just waving a flag on the sidelines waiting for the next opportunity to come along for them?

I honestly believe that we are meant to have friends that are closer than a brother/sibling; friends who love us enough to die for us; stand by us and never throw in the towel because they can see the vision in our hearts.

Know this: that when your vision is for the greater good, the right people will always find their way into your life. I have personally experienced the deception of allowing myself to become too desperate because of the words that were spoken. Another thing to remember, God does give us the desires of our hearts according to His riches in glory. It's His word and this we can depend on as believers.

I quickly learned that sometimes words people speak are as cheap as that same person who speaks them. Be mindful of who you allow speaking into your life and their motives. You can test this theory by the fruit they have already produced and the history of their walk...ask and keep asking. Look out for patterns and understand where they are coming from. If they make you feel like you cannot do anything without their input, yet they have nothing to show for it in their own lives...be wary. If they tell you what they think and criticize you without considering your own positive experiences... be wary. If they undermine your efforts and tell you they know better or have a better way of doing things...be wary if once again they have nothing to show for it. You might be kind, courteous, and generous in all your ways, but you were not made to be someone's doormat. Real friends never take advantage of each other. They are always trying to out give and bless each other; no competition and no keeping scores. They have something called loyalty and wear it proudly on their chest. They respect that you have worked hard to build something with your own hands, and they are going to stick around forever, not drop you when someone more exciting comes along. They keep you in the loop and encourage you to grow so you can become the best version of yourself. They are not deceptive, looking for ways they can take advantage of your kindness. They will protect you and your good name when you are not around. That is love.

I can say this: I'm so saddened when I hear stories of genuinely kind-hearted sisters being taken for. Vulnerability is no joke. As women of God, many of us wear our hearts on our sleeves, so we become sitting ducks for individuals who are looking for opportunities to piggyback off of our success without a second thought. I encourage you, Sister, to cover yourself with the Blood of Jesus and take everything in prayer when it comes to all your relationships. Trust me, you will feel the discomfort of disloyal people in your life and question it, but feel that you are thinking wrongly of that person. It's because of God's pure light and love within you. The darkness or sin cannot stand the light. All things do eventually come into the light and are exposed as they are taken into captivity. We must remember the Holy Spirit and what it means to be a child of God. This is real and God is our comforter and protector by giving us thoughts that guide us away from harm's way, regardless of whether it is a romantic relationship or friendship. I truly believe that's also why God wants us to wait for that special relationship with another believer so we don't have to go through so many emotional disasters testing the waters with people who are not meant to trample our spirits and damage us. If this happens, it would be so easy for us to be pulled away from the plans that God has for our lives; those same plans I've read about are in the Bible that states God wants us to prosper us and not bring harm to us. Plus, the BONUS of that awesome man coming into our lives, who was created in God's image, and is absolutely perfect for us!

So, my dear Sisters in Christ, it's up to us to pay attention to what we are sensing. There really is no other way to describe it as a child of God. We must take all things into prayer so we are never steered wrong by the desires of our hearts, whether it's about fitting in with our peers or finding the perfect guy.

Allow the lessons to be learned. Forgive and release those individuals and then move on. Your pain will heal, and it will also be replaced with joy as you keep hold of your strong faith. I encourage you to embrace the fact that nothing is perfect in this world, but we can find peace, hope, healing, love, friendship, and success in every area of our lives.

The same goes for female friendships. We do connect deeply with our sister friends initially because of emotions in many cases, then we learn quickly what's positive and what's negative about each friendship. Maybe it becomes one-sided. We always have to support them emotionally with every issue that comes up and we stand strong to defend them until one day we realize that the other people were not wrong – our dear sister is unhealed and damaged and we have become an accomplice to their misery and grief. This is a huge eye-opener because we are not narcissistic or vengeful but many things that once seemed fun are staring us in the face and we understand that is not who we are. Or we find ourselves becoming their bank account with too many free withdrawals that never get paid back or they are always borrowing our personal items, such as clothes, shoes, purses, etc.

You see, anytime we have to become vulnerable and trust another, it ultimately seeps into so many other areas of our lives and we find ourselves unexpectantly in icky situations that we were not emotionally prepared to deal with. I have learned in my own journey that it can either become crippling or empowering and this is something that only we can determine for ourselves. Thank goodness God only gives us the lesson until we have learned it and the cycle stops after that. The interesting thing about that is I can clearly remember situations where I had similar experiences with different so-called friendships and I quickly set into motion the quality of my thoughts to that of least resistance. I recognized my patterns and adapted into what kind of outcome I was seeking because I learned very early in life that we cannot change anyone to like us or support us. I realized through so many personal failures and disappointments that people will determine who they want to support and who they want to embrace as their own. I had to be the one who was seeing the best in me. I had to learn to be my own BFF (Best Friend Forever). Please don't get me wrong, I have always had friends and having friends was never an issue in my life because of my outgoing personality. I find joy in everything.

My real friends that truly cared about me listened to my issues, cared about my feelings, understood my pain, brought fun, good memories and lots of great experiences into my life as I also reciprocated it back into their lives. I can honestly say I am thankful for those life-long friendships that remain even though we have grown up and gone our separate ways...I believe we still hold a special place for one another in each other's hearts.

The thing about me was that I also learned this lesson while living it out – you cannot change anyone to like you. You can only change yourself. So, I decided that since I was going to be the only one I could truly depend on, I better start appreciating some things about myself. I better start getting over being Bulimic in high school when only one of my close friends told me that she didn't want me to harm myself any longer. I didn't even know I was doing anything wrong. I just wanted to be skinny. I wanted to be perfect. I wanted to be accepted and liked and popular, which was a next-to-impossible thing to achieve in a small Northwestern Ontario community – I was the ethnic girl; I was the brown girl; I was the black girl. I was the one who didn't fit in. I was the one who stood out. I was the one that my friends who knew and loved me just as I am, couldn't understand why I wanted to be different. You see, when you are part of a small group, you become comfortable. You can feel protected in a sense from the harshness of the world, but in reality, the bigger picture doesn't let you forget. They will still look at you indifferently. They can be in your school, your community groups, even your church. This is life. People will always place you into categories. It will affect your friendships and relationships. I hope this changes for the better, for you.

My younger days were so awesome. I feel I had the best of friends growing up. They never made me feel like an outsider just because I was born in Guyana, South America. However, I recall a time when I had spent a year of Junior high school living in Calgary with relatives to gain a bigger world view. When I returned home at the end of the school year, I felt the shift in how my friends viewed me. Some of them had the struggle to accept me back. Some said I was boasting about my experience. Some said I was just different. You see, in that short time away from my hometown, I quickly understood what was missing from my life and why I felt so trapped and limited. I was a product of my small-town environment who didn't have a world view of who exactly I was in Christ. That had put me in a place of insignificance for so many years. It was the perfect time in my life to actually be exposed to this reality and understand that no matter what others thought of me, their small-minded limiting beliefs about me were just a projection of themselves and I did not ever have to accept it as my own! Talk about a profound awakening! Thank you, Jesus! Unfortunate I had allowed the way others viewed me in a limited capacity to affect so much about who I was growing up to be. Of course, it affected all my relationships and the biggest, most significant relationship was with myself and how I saw who I was. My world expanded and I suddenly saw that I was not the only brown girl in the world. I learned for the first time that being a brown girl was actually beautiful. I was introduced to other brown-skinned friends who loved me exactly as I was, once again. But for some reason, this time it really did feel different and more impactful because we reflected each other in our skins. Now that I've addressed the skin thing, I will admit it is the saddest thing because we miss out on so many beautiful friendships. As for me, my husband is Caucasian, and I see no difference in who he is as my life partner, father of my children, and best friend.

However, the greatest lesson I have learned about female friendships and the vulnerability of opening our hearts to love our friends as sisters is that we all carry preconceived ideas of who our ideal friend is and should be. We hold biases against people without knowing their hearts, motives, the significant impact they could have on our lives, and how we can positively impact theirs. Women, we just role differently amongst each other.

Therefore, as a follower of Christ, it leads me to question if we really understand that the skin thing is a much more serious issue and once we transition from this realm, we are dropping our skins. So, will we even recognize each other in Heaven, if that is our only focus, and not looking at our hearts instead?

Anita Sechesky

You can read Anita's next letter on page 95.

Section Two

Part II

Abundance Mindset

Chapter Ten

SOUL SISTER LETTER
by Rose Marie Young

Dear Sis; My letter today is about having an abundance mindset, which is all about attitude and the way you think. Program your mind to create thoughts that will help enrich your life. These thoughts and ideas should assist you in developing positive actions each and every day. Your mindset should make you feel accomplished and it should give you a sense of appreciation of yourself.

When you have ideas, think big; think outside the normal boundaries.

My dear Soul Sis, position yourself to have abundance in your health, abundance in your wealth, abundance in your business, abundance all your relationships, and abundance in every area of your life.

To have abundance is to have freedom and to live without limitations. The concept of having a positive mind will grow and elevate you not only in your social life, but also in business. It will elevate your self-esteem and by your example, others can be inspired to grow.

An abundance mindset will change your outlook on how you view others and even how you see yourself in a more positive way. You will be able to grow into a courageous, ambitious, and an even more loving person. Be encouraged and be empowered each day by everything you learn and from each experience that you go through. Stay connected always to people with positive feedback, positive attitudes, and energy. Stay positive and be positive. Never forget the keyword – POSITIVE. Having an abundance mindset will help you overcome any obstacle that the enemy sends your way. Be mindful of each decision you make because they will affect your future endeavors and experiences. My dear Sis, I'm telling you that making better choices will give you a more desirable and happier life and it will definitely make your future right. I know for sure that some day you'll see that my words are true. An abundance and positive mindset will even help you sleep better at night; in other words, a stress-free night and a stress-free life. My dear Soul Sister, as you do your makeup, hair, and nails, contemplate what to do each season of each year for the love of God take care of your mind as well. What you think and how you think will definitely affect your future. I hope I'm not being rushed, but it is extremely important that you listen to me.

Keep this letter in a safe place and please refer to it whenever you need to. You'll see and understand what I'm saying when you grow up and mature. Who knows, maybe one day you'll turn out to be just like me.

I suggest to you, my dear Sis, to read as many books as you can because they will help you to expand your mind. As you grow so will your mind. Do not just read books, but also read flyers, posters, and magazines as well. My dear love, I do wish you well as you feed your mind with positive things and good ideas of how to save the planet and this world from itself. Fill your mind with the knowledge that will empower and keep you happy and healthy too.

I know once you're empowered, your life will flourish with abundance as your attitude and ability to think positively will always help to give you new growth.

My dear Soul Sister, I will forever believe in you and don't forget that I love you as well. You should be proud and excited to grow into a great future.

You are wiser than you think. Focus on all that is good in your life. Be thankful and always give back. Helping others will also create abundance in your life. Appreciate the planet and most of all, learn to love. When you love unconditionally and without judgment, you will create positive energy. When you have positive energy, you start tapping into your own source of power, which brings a more positive force.

Do not let any negativity cloud your judgment; always try to do what is right. Put all of your focus on things that make you happy. Surround yourself with people who are positive influencers. These are the people who will help to build your confidence and improve your self-esteem. They can help you to understand what it's like to stay motivated and positive. Do not let the negativity of others discourage you. Never let your fears stop you from progressing into a bright future. Please know that your best self and your best days are yet to be discovered. However, you need to stay strong because a doubtful nature and your own fears can affect you. When you have a change of mind, staying positive will open a lot of doors to success and opportunities. Have better communication, friendships, and collaboration with other positive-minded people, those with an optimistic outlook and positive energy. Their examples will inspire you to walk into your future. You will know what it is to walk in their shoes. Don't be discouraged but believe in yourself. Never think of yourself as a failure or that you are not good enough. Always remember that you, my dear, can choose who you will become. Always try to be the best in everything you do. Try to find the best in everyone around you. Never give up on yourself. If you attempt something and it doesn't work out, keep striving. If it's God's will for you to do something, it will be done. He will make a way for you to succeed. He will give you strength and knowledge. He knows everything you need to help you succeed in this world. Just keep your mindset in the right place and stay positive.

Don't be discouraged by the negative feedback from others who are not supportive nor believe in your dreams. They may not want to see you succeed while others may not want to see you grow up and be filled with great achievements. They may try to hold you back from going forward. Be true to yourself. Keep believing that you are capable, you are determined, and you never give up. Again, I really appreciate you and I believe that God blessed the earth on the very day of your birth. Your mindset and focus may change with time because of the many variations in the environment and the world around you. When this happens, don't give up. Confusion can help you to grow into a stronger and more empowered woman. Another thing I'd like to say is don't be in such a hurry to reach the top or to conquer the world: it can wait for you. Empower your mind and be enlightened to know that you are the product of a God of wisdom and abundance.

You are a very critical and important part of God's plan. Everything that God has ordained for you will be received in due time. Be patient and believe that you can achieve everything that you put your mind to. Do not let anyone's negative forces discourage you, for you are a brave soul. Having an abundance mindset will help you transform into your true divine purpose.

My dearest Soul Sister, I do not want you to miss anything. Life is full of so much excitement and great adventure. Enjoy all the good things nature has for you to see. Be fascinated by new things. Don't be afraid of anything that you may encounter.

You deserve to be all that you can. So, don't just sit back and become stressed out about loosing even a dime. Please believe me when I say I have experienced many distrustful situations. I lost many things as well. However, none of them were attached to my body or were part of my being. I became momentarily discouraged, but with my abundance mindset I quickly changed my outlook. Those material things are never really a part of the true me. Do not let them distract you from your greater goals. As the saying goes, nothing lasts forever.

If you keep your focus on the right things in life, you'll see that when stuff happens, you my friend will be already armed with the confidence to face any challenge. Do not hesitate and stress over the little small things. Use your abundance mindset to create a legacy of excellence and great success. You are a woman of divine splendor – celebrate your beautiful Life.

Your mind is one of the most powerful tools. Don't just use it to create nor store information that doesn't excel you. The maintenance of your mind is important and needs to be empty of all negativity. Use your mind to bring healing into a lost world of brokenness. Remember that you are here for a purpose; use your mind to bring hope to others. Always be an encouragement and inspiration to everyone you meet.

As I mentioned in one of my letters, some people may try to influence you the wrong way, but with your mindset and your great abilities of discernment, they will not be able to affect you. With your mindset, you'll never have to stay behind as a follower because you will be a great leader. You, my Sis, were born to be a trailblazer. Please respect others and always shows compassion. Be kind and thoughtful. If you believe in someone, show it; hey will respect you. Do not be quick to judge those who are different than you or those you do not understand. People are different and special in their own unique ways. Respect the laws of the universe, such as "Do unto others as you would have others do unto you."

God created goodness in you, so be good to others and never forget to always be good to yourself.

We are always growing and learning. To maintain a positive and more abundant mindset, you should always stay connected with a higher source of knowledge. That main and higher source is God. He is the ever-knowing Creator. Stay connected with others who believe in Him, however, take time to have a personal one on one with him each day. Please read more in my last letter.

My point is, as my Soul Sister, I want to encourage you to keep your mind focused on the best things this life has to offer. Each of us is given one life and one life only, so cherish it. Have fun and enjoy it. Learn more and more with all your many experiences, but do not be consumed by a small and limited mindset. Take charge of situations that seen to bring your energy down. Embrace every opportunity where there are changes. Own those changes, learn from them, and create positive outcomes. Use them as your stepping stones for growth. Don't forget to help others to grow through better understandings of themselves. Always share your knowledge to help others overcome. The more you share, the more you will gain. There is enough abundance for everyone.

My friend and Soul Sister, I just want to let you know that it's okay to think big and always want more for yourself. Always be optimistic and know that the best is yet to come. Strive for excellence at all times and always make your better the best. Stay driven, be open-minded, and be flexible to new ideas and new adventures. With each new achievement and success, it's okay to celebrate but don't forget to recognize everyone else who have helped you and have been there for you. Acknowledge those who have stepped forward to appreciate you and to applaud your success with you. When things go wrong, as they sometimes do, know there's hope and you will get another shot. From my experience, success is failure turned inside out. Be optimistic and know that when one door closes, another one will open. God will send someone to help you stand strong.

Abundance mindset means never giving up. Always stay hopeful and know that there is something better waiting to be discovered by you. A positive mindset also means believing in miracles and most often those miracles are related directly to your dreams, your ambitions, and the stillness of that beautiful picture you created in your mind. Go ahead, my Soul Sister, and take chances on your dreams. Create and build the beautiful life that your heart desires. Do not limit your access to great abundance.

Dream the biggest dream.

Rose Marie Young

You can read Rose's next letter on page 103.

Abundance is my birthright as a child of God. I accept every blessing that has my name on it.

—Anita Sechesky

SOUL SISTER LETTER
by Koreen Bennett

Dear Sis; I believe that we should always look to God because we are all beautifully created in his image, and with God, we can do all things. Positive mindset: what do I say about that, Sisters? I would say to my younger self, "Hey baby girl, I love you!" To all my sisters, love yourself and loving yourself means telling yourself that you're beautiful, you're smart, you have the prettiest smile, you have the biggest brown eyes/blue eyes/green eyes (you put in whatever eye color you have). I would say to you that I love the freckles on your cheeks; your lips are big, some would say, but guess what? God made them that way so when you give kisses, they will be unforgettable. Your hair is beautiful, your strength, and no one can wear your hair like you can. You're strong-willed, you're powerful, you're a Boss lady. You know what, Sister? I'm going to ask you right now! Wherever you are! Yeah! Even if you're standing in the middle of a supermarket, I want you to hug yourself. I'm serious!! Hug yourself and say to yourself, "I've got you, girl." I would say most of us are quick to see our failures over our accomplishments. Why is that? It takes one thought or a phone call to shift your thought process. It takes that one person you work with to inject a negative word, it gets into your head, and POOF! We have now allowed that person, that hurtful comment or words, to penetrate our thought process and it's OVER. I say we need to take back our power and tell the enemy, "BACK OFF! Not getting in my head today or ever!"

I am at a place in my life right now where reading, listening to audiobooks, or watching videos that focus on my mindset is a requirement. Social media can be tricky but again you have control over what you take in. I have to be a lifetime athlete and that just means I need to train, not only my body, but I need to train my brain (did you know it's a muscle?) because it is easy to fall back into old habits and old ways of thinking. I have to make sure that my surroundings are positive and the people who are in my circle are abundance focused and positive-minded. I've dealt with comments and words that have brought me hurt and have broken my spirit. It is the hardest thing to remove a negative comment or comments that have been spoken into your ears for years. The good thing is that it's possible to reverse that situation. Don't listen to the naysayers. I had to seek the Lord and look for people who spoke positive and surrounded myself with them; people who talked and walked positivity. Having a positive mindset allows you to talk and walk with confidence. It is that confidence in knowing who you are and whose you are. The Lord God made you and you are Fearfully and Wonderfully made, my Sister friend. I encourage you – don't take everybody into your heart and headspace because not everybody has the right to be there. I say if a sentence or a comment starts off with a negative word or negative tone, I give you permission to put your hands over your ears and block that (hopefully, with you doing that, whoever is speaking to you will get the message). Speak positively into your life. Stand in front of the mirror and tell yourself that today is a great day. Today is MY day that the Lord God has made, and I will rejoice and be glad in it. Speak to yourself; speak over your life daily affirmations. That's how you keep that positive mindset. Read self-development books that will pour positiveness into yourself. You will come across people (family, friends, sisters) who will intentionally or unintentionally say a negative comment or speak words of negativity. You have the power to say, "NO! I don't need or want that around me." A positive mindset requires positive personal space and surroundings.

As a nurse, I would love to speak with my residents and ask them about their younger days. Those who could recollect would have beautiful stories to share. Encouraging them and reminding them of their worth would ignite a joy; the smile would get bigger; they would have more stories to tell me. So, if they were having a not-so-good day, it changed in that moment. Now things may not change overnight, and for me, it took years to remove a lot of negative thoughts as it took years to get there, so be patient with yourself. Yes. I took many steps forward and as many steps backward, but I worked on my self every day. It was also easy to hang out with the "negative cheerleaders" as misery loves company, but I became intentional, focused, and with lots of prayers and doing little things like reading my bible, again listening to positive videos, reading daily positive affirmations, writing them on my mirror, on paper, and sticking them on the walls or anywhere, it was in my face constantly. That is what I had to do for a while, and I still write things on my mirror to keep me in that headspace. We do need to have a tunnel vision, sisters. We are juggling many things. We know that our minds and emotions do go all over the place at times, most times, and we know that there is an enemy who is just waiting to steal your thoughts (battling for your mind), but I want you to know that you are strong, you are mighty, and if you keep speaking the Word every day, you will be strengthened in such a way that you won't believe it was a struggle before. My nightly routine now is after I say my prayers, I fall asleep listening to a motivational speaker or one of my favorite preachers. It has to be something that nourishes my mind and keeps my thoughts in a positive place.

Thinking abundance is not just about having things. It's having the mindset that I can achieve anything I desire. Do you have an abundance mindset or a scarcity mindset? An abundance mindset says there is a huge field out there for everyone to pick from. There will always be more than enough. Just imagine the sky full of stars. A field completely covered in corn stalks or sunflowers. There is a vast amount for everyone and to anyone who wants of it. It's how I look at life now. There are countless opportunities out there for you and me. I believe you can have an abundance of loving people in your circle; you can an abundance of ideas and money. I also believe that it's my responsibility and yours as well to have a positive abundant mindset. I choose to live an abundant life for me and my family, but it first had to start in my head. I had to change my mindset. I had to change the way I looked at things and people. I want to change my world and those that I come into contact with for the better. I want to be a successful entrepreneur; I want to be a great wife, mother, and grandmother. I believe I Can, and I Will. Remember, Sis, a positive abundant mindset is developed. I will say it again: positive talks to yourself will help you stay in a positive abundant mindset. **FIRST THING IN THE MORNING**, as this sets the tone for the rest of your day, throughout the day, and **BEFORE GOING TO BED**. Instead of worrying, repeating that negative thought or how your day might have turned out how you wanted it to (as I use to do), speak little positive statements or even one or two words like "I AM STRONG! I AM BOLD! I AM BLESSED! I CAN DO IT!" to yourself. It will make a difference. This will take time. It is a process and will not happen in a snap of your finger. I had to, in a way, reprogram myself and the way I spoke to myself and others during conversation. I know now that this is a daily walk and talk for me. I constantly read something positive and I listen to something positive as it is easy to fall back into previous practices.

So, I say to you, "Believe that you can achieve it and you will." Believe that you are successful, speak it, and see if things change around you. Spend every day speaking to yourself health, prosperity, love, wealth.

> *"The Lord is my Shepherd. I shall not want."* Psalm 23:1

> *"The Joy of the Lord is My Strength."* Nehemiah 8:10

> *"For God has not given us a spirit of fear, but of power and of love and of a sound mind."* 2 Timothy 1:7 (NKJV)

You can accomplish anything you put your mind to as you continue to develop your positive abundant mindset. As we persevere on our journey, I believe that our mindset change will inspire, encourage, and empower us.

"There is nothing as powerful as a changed mind" - T.D. Jakes

O Lord, fill _____ with the Spirit of God, in Wisdom, Understanding, in Knowledge, and use the gifts that you have given them for your Glory. Amen.

Koreen Bennett

You can read Koreen's next letter on page 111.

SOUL SISTER LETTER
by Dominique Dunn Malloy

God has not given me a spirit of fear, but of power, love, and a sound mind. 2 Timothy 1:7 (KJV)

Whatsoever things are true, whatsoever things are honest, whatsoever things are just, whatsoever things are pure, whatsoever things are lovely, whatsoever things are of good report; if there be any virtue, and if there be any praise, think on these things. Philippians 4:8 (KJV)

Dear Sis; You may have hit a roadblock in life, a spot where you think it's time to throw in the towel. You may have heard the alarm ring in your ear and groaned as you slapped the snooze button, pulled the covers over your head, and rolled over to go back to sleep because you thought life was too sad to live through. Well, sister, you are not alone. I know I've done that many days in the last several years because sometimes it's not easy facing reality, but let me share with you something I have learned in my journey of grief. After my mom passed away just a few short years, I got a glimpse of how my mother struggled in my adolescent years as she battled with her own thoughts because I had watched her waste away. A year after letting myself sink deep into despair in reaction to her passing, I decided to make a shift in my mind to regain my strength and to get back to being the master of my world. I had wasted too much time in self-pity, doubt, and self-loathing. I realized if I kept going down the path I was on, it would not just be destructive to myself but to my husband, my family, and all the lives around me I no longer paid attention to. I was essentially on the same trajectory as my late mother in her later years: sad, lonely, and depressed. So, I had to make a decision. Do I let grief, sadness, and hurt eat me up? Or do I daily choose to take action by focusing on my values, my integrity, and my own happiness because it is in your inner world that you dictate to your outer world? I watched growing up this exact destructive film playing for my mother, so I knew what it looked like if I continued to live in blame and self-pity. As long as I allowed myself to feel those emotions, I gave them power over me. This was the point where God picked me up, dusted me off, and reminded me that if I wanted more, I had to become more. If I wanted happiness, I had to choose happiness; not just once but daily.

This perpetual routine of love and admiration was something I tried hard to do on a daily basis for my husband and others, but I forgot to do it for myself. This was made evident to me one morning when I looked into our bathroom mirror a few days after one of his recent birthdays. I had filled the mirror with my daily affirmations to him. They read: "Did I tell you today I Love you." "I'm proud of you." "I appreciate you." "You're insanely brilliant." "I'm so lucky to be the girl by your side." As I looked at these sticky notes on the mirror, I realized that although daily I would try to be intentional about saying these things to him, I rarely ever said these to myself anymore.

If you're in a spot where you may not be thoroughly enjoying life, I can tell you that you're not alone and I want to assure you there is absolutely nothing wrong with you. So, you may ask where we go from here? Well, it usually begins with how you perceive the world to be. Everything can change for the better when you shift your perspective about how you are looking at the situation at hand. When my mother passed, I was engulfed by feelings of victimhood thinking only of myself and of the lack that surrounded me. As a result of that mindset, that's all that could come back into my life: lack and limitation. But when I switched my perspective as I did in the years prior, when I thought I hit rock bottom from a scarcity mindset to an abundance mentality, I knew my life could be changed in an instant.

Therefore, as you can see it all starts with you accepting yourself and being aware of your thoughts, emotions, and actions. The biggest lesson I can pass on to you in this regard is to be true to your integrity, not only with others but with yourself. Consequently enough, I could always have integrity with others where, on the contrary, I could not do it with myself. When I learned to do what I told myself I was going to do, I started to enjoy myself once again as I did so many years ago.

I'm going to take you back to just a few months ago to tell you about a habit that I have been working on overcoming and now I believe I have mastered. Have you ever blamed someone else and zoned in on their flaws because you couldn't look at yourself? You knew you weren't doing enough or living to your truest potential? Well, that's exactly what I found myself doing to my dear boyfriend. I would get so caught up looking outside of myself rather than inside. I was always someone who pushed herself to be better, however, sometimes it's a lot easier looking at others than it is looking oneself. For this reason, if you are in any relationship with someone who is not treating you the best, know that it's not a reflection on you. Most of the time it's a deeper problem within the person afflicting the pain.

What I did not understand was that in pushing myself, I forgot to love myself. This is where having incredible integrity by keeping your word to yourself really helps build that love and admiration for the woman you are growing into. When you learn to have inner peace and accept who you are, you're able to show up not only authentically but powerfully. This is what an abundance mindset will give you: freedom as well as courage to live your best life because rather than thinking of what you're lacking (and attracting lack), you will attract love and greater abundance. If you look for the greater things in life, they will present themselves to you before you know it.

Dominique Dunn Malloy

You can read Dominique's next letter on page 115.

SOUL SISTER LETTER
by Anita Sechesky

Dear Sis; How's it going in the manifestation department lately? Have you been limiting yourself in how you see life? Don't despair because it's not too late for you to shift the way you are allowing life's blessings from passing you by.

As a Law of Attraction practitioner, I can tell you that everything begins with your thoughts. So, if your thoughts are tainted with deep roots of discouragement from past failures or rejection, more than likely you are still struggling with self-esteem and how you show up in the world.

Firstly, let me point you to scripture:

> *"And my God will supply every need of yours according to his riches in glory in Christ Jesus."* Philippians 4:19 (EVS)

> *"For I know the plans I have for you, declares the Lord, plans for welfare and not for evil, to give you a future and a hope."* Jeremiah 29:11 (ESV)

> *"Blessed is the man who walks not in the counsel of the wicked, nor stands in the way of sinners, nor sits in the seat of scoffers, but his delight is in the law of the Lord, and on his law, he*

meditates day and night. He is like a tree planted by streams of water that yields its fruit in its season, and its leaf does not wither. In all that he does, he prospers." Psalm 1:1-3 (ESV)

My Sisters, there are literally hundreds of passages in the Holy Bible that indicate we are blessed and have access to all the blessings that God has prepared for us as his children.

So why do we keep thinking otherwise? Why do we struggle? Why do we lack? Are we being punished?

I have asked myself these same questions so many times, and then God brings to remembrance that sweet solid truth that yes, God has called me as His very own. But it's the sin in my life that's actually blocking my blessings. This prompts me in the busyness of my life to wake up and take notice that once again in my weak humanness, I stepped out of God's will for my life failing to repent and asking forgiveness. Even forgiving others who have wronged me may have opened the door of sin in my life because I started harboring ill feelings against someone. It is so easy to not walk a righteous life and yet it just as easy to walk joyfully in the presence of the Lord. I say this boldly knowing my own shortcomings and personal attitude when it comes to the Abundance mindset. We tend to shift our focus and look to others who are at the top of their game. Success seems to follow them so easily and we wonder what's wrong with us? Why is it always this way?

I have personally learned the biggest game-changer is when we realize what we focus on is literally what we are attracting into our lives. For example, what are you feeding your mind on a daily basis? Who are you listening to? Who are you following on social media? Whose books are you reading? When was the last time you did any kind of personal growth training? Have you processed and released all your emotional baggage?

Let's break it down so we can examine ourselves in a productive way.

If I asked you what you do on a daily basis in the morning, what category would you fit into?

- read scripture devotionals
- listen to worship music
- get into prayer mode and lay it all on the cross
- declare blessings over my household

What we feed our minds and the secret to our success is always found in our daily routines.

I encourage you to reflect on this momentarily and if you know you have been procrastinating and then complaining or holding negative thoughts inside because you wish you were living differently, it's not too late. Forgive yourself and release all forms of malice towards anyone in your life that you may actually be jealous of. Instead, start looking at everyone and everything differently because old stagnant emotions will keep attracting itself back into your life. You want to take that trash out as soon as you are consciously aware of it. You will then notice that your energy will shift because you are looking through different lenses. You see, once you recognize that God is no respecter of person and what He has done for others, He can also do for you, you will realize that no one is better than another. Jesus died for all of our sins, not just your neighbor across the street. Your life is just as valuable and important. So that means the quality of your life as well. God wants us all to prosper and be of good health. The bible says that he wants us to prosper as our souls prosper. I believe God's word to be true and acceptable in my life. I am well aware of my humanity and where I fall short because of my lack of seeking God in all my ways. I know it always feels heavy and uncomfortable if I allow myself to become jealous or spiteful. We are not immune to these feelings, but it's also our responsibility to put these thoughts into immediate captivity and not let them run rampant in our minds, which is our greatest battle. The enemy of our souls may plant seeds of contempt against others and because of our vulnerability by not clearing our minds and building our faith in prayer, we are prone to going down a rabbit hole of sin and with that usually comes discouragement in many forms.

I believe we tend to make things so much more difficult than our Heavenly Father intended things to be. We have issues with trust and as a result, because we do not see a physical God before us, we easily slip up and forget that because of the very fact that God is not a man, He will not lie to us.

> *"God is not a man, that he should lie; Neither the son of man, that he should repent: hath he said and shall he not do it?"*
> Numbers 23:19 (KJV)

It's time for us all to stand on God's word and meditate on it for what it is: B - basic, I - information, B - before, L - leaving, E - earth.

An interesting thing about life as a Christian: it's often been said that life doesn't come with a manual, but as a child of God, we hold contrary to that statement as we have access to the Keys of the Kingdom living. This means as joint heirs in Christ Jesus, as children of God, we are abundantly blessed whether we believe it or not. It's our inheritance and it's time we start living as just so. We must cast off all vain imaginations and trust God's word as it is. We must recognize that to reap good fruit we must sow into good soil. We must fertilize our body, mind, and spirt on the Word and promises of God. We must forgive often and release all sin that tries to stick itself onto us.

We can definitely do all things through Christ, but do we actually believe this to be true? If I were to observe you, what would I see? Are you confident? Are you generous? Are you thinking of the needs of others? Do you sow love and blessings in every life you are connected with?

I encourage you, Sis, to continually clean your mind of all the things that have not edified your beautiful soul. Release all the words that have been spoken over any kind of success or prosperity in your life. Forgive every single person who has ever betrayed your trust. Process the steps over and ask God to forgive you for not putting your complete trust and hope in Him.

My prayer for you is that you will rise up when you feel like falling.

> Forgive when you give in.
>
> Release when you want to hold onto to negativity.
>
> As you clean up your spirit, you heal up your emotional wounds.
>
> As you process your pain in the light of understanding, what was sent to destroy you cannot harm you – if you release it completely to God.
>
> As you release all the bad, hurtful, destructive words spoken over your life, I pray you begin to feel the heaviness of sin move away from you.
>
> As you repent for your weakness of questioning God's promises for you, I believe blessings will begin to be activated within you.
>
> As you see everyone equally, you will appreciate that everything is also for you.
>
> As you let go of feelings of rejection, you will remember that Christ died just for you. In doing so, He unlocked so many more blessings just for you.
>
> As you recognize that there is no need to feel insignificant, unrepresented, denied, damaged, less than, inferior, or unappreciated, you will see the contrast of how special you really are.

I pray that you will finally let go of all the repressed emotions of unworthiness and of low standards; that the God of all truth will be able to heal what is hurting deep inside of you. We have not because we ask not. We settle and hurt ourselves because we fail to step forward in faith and receive the unconditional love God our Heavenly Father has for us. Sometimes we forget that as we reject God's love, we are also rejecting Christ's death on the cross in which He so willingly died without question, and without sin. He knew us who are full of so much sin, yet He gave His life up just for our redemption, salvation, healing, restoration, and victory over so many things we actually struggle with on a daily basis. Abundant living is one of the most common ones; many church folks fail to walk in daily. Please stop this madness of what the Israelites did for forty years, yet in their lesson, they still did not see how God loved them so much. Their shoes never wore out, they never hungered or cried out for thirst. God showed us through their lives how much He loves his children. This is endless, unconditional love...who are we to deny the blessings. God's words say:

> *"Ask, and it shall be given you; seek, and ye shall find; knock, and it shall be opened unto you. For everyone that asketh receiveth; and he that seeketh findeth, and to him that knocketh it shall be opened."* Matthew 7:7-8 (KJV)

This, my Sisters, is your answer to having an Abundant Mindset in Christ.

Anita Sechesky

You can read Anita's next letter on page 121.

Section Two

Part III
Divine Purpose

Unconditional love begins with you. If you want love, you must be Love in action.

—Anita Sechesky

SOUL SISTER LETTER
by Rose Marie Young

Dear Sis; I'm starting off this letter to you with a few words that have been written in the Bible.

For you created my inmost being;
you knit me together in my mother's womb.
I praise you because I am fearfully and wonderfully made;
your works are wonderful,
I know that full well.
My frame was not hidden from you
when I was made in the secret place,
when I was woven together in the depths of the earth.
Your eyes saw my unformed body;
all the days ordained for me were written in your book
before one of them came to be. (Psalm 139, 13-16)

Always remember, my dear Sister, that you are a child of God. Knowing this will help you understand who you really are. You have a Divine Purpose which is a gift from The Creator himself. It is a special assignment that each of us has been given by God to do while we are in the world. These gifts are what we use to inspire, to motivate, and to bring healing to one another. Your Divine purpose will not only bring healing to others, but it will also help you live and enjoy a better and more meaningful life. A Divine Purpose is what gives each of us an individual fulfillment and joy. When you discover what your purpose is, you will find it makes a great difference in everything you do. For example, how you treat yourself and how you treat others. It will also make a difference in the choices and decisions you make. When you believe that you are a child of God, you find Freedom in knowing that He will always be there for you. It's good to be reassured knowing that He's there in your going out and in your arrival to and from anywhere. God is even in our thoughts and in our deeds. He is that very small voice in your mind that lets you know when things are not right or when you are about to do something wrong. He is that small voice that speaks calmness and peace to your soul. Whenever you are troubled, in Him you will find peace. Most of all, you will find affection, and furthermore, when you do His will, His abundance of blessings will flow in your life.

You are armored with Divine protection and given a sense of love and peace to help you discover your true self. This will enable you and gives you courage while you are finding your purpose. It can sometimes be hard because of the many different choices and directions you have. Discovering your true purpose can be extremely overwhelming. As you try each day to understand what you are searching for, you will see evidence in your life of what your specific assignment is. This is your purpose.

Things are always happening around you, and as you are growing so is the world around you. With each phase of your growth, you will learn that you are stepping more into your Divine purpose. Each experience will directly or indirectly help you to become connected spiritually with God. A spiritual relationship with God and a spiritual pilgrimage will prepare you for your true purpose. It's important to have a vision of where you need to go and who you want to be.

Sometimes we have to learn to explore and experience different things in our lives and take certain measures to ensure achieve our goals. God wants us to be of service to Him. He needs to prepare us so He can begin to use us as His shepherds for His glory. A doctor has to be trained and educated for several years before they can begin performing surgery.

My dear Sister, whatever it is that you choose to do, whatever your dreams are, God has a specific purpose for you. You should know that He wants to bless you as well as use you to bless others with the gifts he has given you. You should be wise and know whatever His will is for you, it will be. Open your mind and receive his gifts. You were chosen before you were in your mother's womb.

There are going to be times in your life that you're going to be tested. These tests are for you to learn from and therefore become your best possible self. Make choices but choose well. Not all gifts are from God. Don't worry if you don't fit in and don't be angry if your gift is different from others. Each of our assignments is different and that's what makes us special and unique individuals. Understand the lessons learned from your past experiences. The knowledge that you gained from all that you have encountered will help you when you find your true self and purpose.

My dear Sis, on a quest to find your true calling, ask God to give you a revelation to enlighten you as you journey into your future. I know that each of us has our own destiny and calling. Ask God to direct you and to show what to do. Follow His guidance. He will direct you to the right people who need your help and he will connect you to the right people who will help you. You can be very committed to serving in different areas of your community and in the world. Do not hesitate to contact others who have other gifts that you can identify with. Devotion and thanksgiving are all part of serving. It is imperative that you implement them in your daily life. When you fully devote yourself to accomplishing your goals, you are able to become focused. Owning your calling as a leader and as a servant of God, you will be also encouraged to take on other assignments. This gives you confirmation that because you are committed to serving God, He rewards you by giving you other assignments and increasing your blessings.

My dear Sis, I want you to be passionate about your gifts. Be happy and thankful. Your purpose is something that makes you unique and makes you stand out above the crowd. Appreciate it and be proud.

Everyone has a gift that they were given. To me, my special gift is love, for myself and everyone in the world. My Soul Sister, I just want to say before I end this letter that I love you. Life can be filled with palpable emotions, but nevertheless, we should be thankful for all the blessed talents that we were given. Whatever you do for a brother or for another sister, please do it from your heart and from a place of love.

Although we all have special assignment purposes, we were created to transmit an abundance of Love and Joy to the world. When we transfer love, we create unity. So, my dear Soul Sister, I'm going to challenge you to spread some love to everyone that you will meet today. If it's only a smile, that will be fine because one of our Divine purposes is to share the love and to be kind. Be love; be peace; and be blessed by God himself with an abundance as you live your life by Faith to be an ambassador for God. Learn what's important when you're an ambassador for God. It's very necessary to build relationships and invest in them personally. It's important that you value others, their opinions, and their ideas. Their opinions can be different from yours but be respectful and support others in their endeavors to accomplish their goals. Be aware of your emotions. Balance them with your words and your actions. Your focus should always be on your mission and connect yourself with others who are like-minded as you. Don't be afraid to take the initiative to genuinely connect.

Practice good discipline skills. Also, set virtuous examples so others can follow in your footsteps. Always be accountable for your own actions. Never be too afraid to ask for forgiveness or too proud to forgive others. As mentioned, one of your Divine purposes is to love. To love is to forgive. When you forgive, you can find freedom. To be free is to have peace in your soul.

My Soul Sister, I advise you to forgive those who have wronged you that you may find peace in your soul. Make it your mission to be fully devoted to your quest to find your purpose. God expects us to develop and use the gifts he gives us. Be motivated and enthusiastic about yourself and your accomplishments. Challenge yourself each day to use your purpose, which is your gift, for good. Inspire others and pray daily; it is like a report and also accountability to your Heavenly Father. Always be passionate about making the investment to prove your gifts even if it's a financial investment. Pray not only for yourself but pray for others as well. Stay informed so you can improve your special gifts. Take time out of your busy day to share with other people the blessings that you are given. Try doing something that gives you fulfillment. And finally, my dear soul sister, read the Bible daily. From it, you'll draw strength to encourage yourself when you are in difficulty to protect yourself and your precious gifts from the adversaries.

We are all faced with challenges. However, we are created equally but with different personalities. Each gift that is given to us is directly associated with our personalities. What's your special gift? Does it match your personality? Some people have been given the gift of teaching. Some have been given the gift of music. Some, healing. Some are given the gift to cook or to be a mother. Others are given the gift of administration, and so on.

These are roles that we are responsible to render our services in. When you are given a specific individual talent, manage and execute it by following guidelines on how to be empowered by it. Take your leadership seriously. Gain knowledge and education yourself to fully understand your role and how it intertwines with everything in this big world. Be mindful of others whose roles and purposes may be different from yours: they are just as important. Always remember that we are only part of a bigger picture. and we are all connected spiritually in some ways or another. And because we are connected to one God, our purposes are interwoven together to serve, love, and glorify God.

My dear Soul Sister, I requested you to take everything I've written in this letter and make it applicable to your own life. Discover your purpose, become inspired to accomplish your own success, and reach new heights by using the gifts that God has blessed you with. Overcome the challenges that life may bring. Try to find comfort and peace in your heart by using the gift of forgiveness. Take charge of your future but do not concern yourself with the past. Submit yourself to God so he can use you for His glory. Walk in love and demonstrate that to others by example. Respect yourself always as a believer in God just as He has an abundance of blessings in store for you. God needs you to trust him. The gifts you have been given are also testing you to see how you're able to handle them, use them, and how much you appreciate them. Always use the gifts that God has given you for good and not for evil purposes.

Let me warn you to never be envious or jealous of another person's gifts. Focus on your own, live with integrity, and never lose your ambition while you are riding on the ship of success. Be very dignified in your conduct. Walk in respect, walk in wisdom, and walk in love.

My Soul Sister, I want you to know that your pure, true love is a reflection of God's own image. He has purposely chosen you for His own purpose. Some of the many things you have felt and dealt with in the past have prepared you to meet this exciting future. I believe that this was God's plan all along. *"For I know the plans I have for you," declares the Lord, plans to prosper you and not to harm you, plans to give you hope and a future."* Jeremiah 29:11 (NIV)

Yesterday is gone. Leave the past behind and start enjoying your bright new future. You're talented and brave. God would not have chosen you for this purpose if He thought for a moment that you, my dear, could not survive. You are a perfect fit for these gifts. My love, your best days are right in front of you. You have a purpose.

I know as you are serving God to fulfill your purpose, you will for His sake take care of yourself as well. As you recall, one of our many purposes is to love one another and to love ourselves. Please remember that self-love and self-development are very important to our overall health and success.

Rose Marie Young

You can read Rose's next letter on page 127.

Chapter Fifteen

SOUL SISTER LETTER
by Koreen Bennett

Dear Sis; I believe I was created to leave a great impact on this generation, and I believe the same for you. God is in your life to fulfill His vision. I would love to share with you why I feel in my spirit that we should inspire, encourage, and empower one another at all times. Just before I comment, I would like to read this scripture; Jeremiah 29 verse 11, says *"For I know the thoughts I think towards you, says the Lord. Thoughts of peace and not of evil, to give you a future and a hope."* I really do believe that we are created for a reason; we all have a purpose. I find as I am sitting here in front of my computer, I'm wondering, "What is it that I can tell you? What can I say to my sisters, the girl, the woman who's reading this chapter?" Have you ever sat and wondered what your purpose is? Or, you see someone just achieving and walking in their gifting and wonder, "When am I going to know what I want to do? When will I understand my calling? What am I passionate about?"

I believe with all my heart that God has a MASTERPLAN FOR YOU and ME. It took me a while to figure out my passion, my divine purpose. I believe it was always there inside of me, but I just did not activate it. I didn't really tap into what God had planted inside me. I believe it is good to have mentors; people who don't have an agenda but really want to see you succeed. I now pray for God to send specific mentors and coaches into my life to assist with nurturing and guiding my giftings, especially if I am still trying to understand what God has given me. God has something specific for us to do while we're on this earth and as I sit here thinking what I should say to my sisters regarding these two words, I would first tell you to find out what your divine purpose is. Find your passion, that thing that won't leave you alone until you fulfill it. I would seek the Lord and I would ask Him what it is. Why am I here? What is my purpose? Why was I created? How can I be a solution? What problems are out there that I can bring a solution to? I believe this is something that many of us girls struggle with, but again it is first seeking your Creator, looking at your heart, and asking yourself what you would love to do to help someone else. How much of a burden is it when you're doing something, working somewhere, and it's not your heart's desire? It's not what's giving you fulfillment. When your life is assigned to a purpose, nothing can stop you. Am I being a solution to a problem? Am I a problem solver? Am I making someone's life better just because of my presence? God has empowered you and I, but we are not using the power if it's not activated. I would say to my younger self and to my sisters out there, "I encourage you to seek out your purpose and God will show you your divine purpose. I believe you were born for something special. I empower you to find the real you, the true you and to be a solution for someone out there whether it be in your inner circle, on your job, in your church, in a support group, in sports, or a reading club."

It took me years to figure out God's divine purpose for me. I struggled with low self-worth and low self-esteem for many years. Carrying that with you for years can bring self-hatred, closes you off to relationships, closes you off to opportunities, especially understanding and walking in your divine purpose, and so I had to get to a place where I asked God, "Who am I? Why am I here?

Why was I really created?" I didn't see me being of any value to myself, much less to someone else and how could I help someone else when I could hardly help myself. I could barely encourage and inspire myself, so how could I encourage, inspire, and empower others when I couldn't do it for myself. Of course, this was a process; it was no overnight makeover for me, but when I realized how much love I had to give and how much I had to share, I believed at that moment I had an understanding of my divine purpose. I decided that I needed to follow through and become what God said I was and would be. By nature, I am a nurturer, a caregiver, and heart-centered. That is why I was chosen to be a Registered Nurse (yes, I did the work, went to school, but I did not come up with the idea. That was placed in my spirit, but I didn't understand it then).

When I think back to my childhood, I spoke into existence what was in my heart. I was always the teacher or the nurse when I played childhood games with my siblings. As I am writing this letter to you, I am getting many revelations that I didn't connect until now. Even contributing to this book is part of my divine purpose. I dreamt of writing, but I thought it would be a book with poems in it. So, back to nursing. That has been my heart's desire for years. I always wanted to help, bring joy, and put a smile on peoples' faces. When someone was in pain, it was as if I felt that person's pain. I'm sure there's another person out there just like me. Maybe there's one other girl out there who's feeling the same way I'm feeling; I would want to know that person out there felt the same way I did, and I would want to know how she did it. Sometimes you find your purpose when you are in the lowest of lows. Sometimes you get inspired and you just get it. I hope the gifts that my Lord has given me will be shared with others I know and don't know. I hope that you and I will leave an impact on this world. I hope that in my sharing, you will feel and see your sense of purpose, value, and significance.

Sister, your Heavenly Father has a purpose for your life. I encourage you to seek God out. Find a quiet place, call out to Him, let God know that you are ready for Him to show you why He created you, and allow Him to tell you how beautiful you are. You are Important. You are Needed. You are Powerful. I believe you, my sister-friend, are definitely here for a time as this. And you are Fearfully and Wonderfully made. I say to put on your Crown of Royalty because you are a daughter of the King. The gift that you carry is pure, and not duplicated. Only you can possess it. You will inspire many. *"Success is a result of a decision. Failure is a result of decisions"* - Dr. Myles Munroe. You are very special to the Lord. Love him with all your heart and He will direct your every footstep. Sisters. Please. I ask you to follow your purpose-driven life. Fulfill Your Gift. You are Chosen. You are carrying something valuable and it is needed to Impact the Nation. I speak blessings over you, Sister. You are on your way to your destination – Destiny.

Koreen Bennett

You can read Koreen's next letter on page 135.

SOUL SISTER LETTER
by Dominique Dunn Malloy

I will make you into a great nation, and I will bless you; I will make your name great, and you will be a blessing. Genesis 12:2

Dear Sis; Let's talk about a purpose-driven life. Have you discovered what your purpose to life is yet? Or are you still searching for its beauty to surround you? They say the two most important days of your life are: the day you were born and the day you realize why. I was incredibly empowered when I found my distinct purpose in life. It opened the doors to so many unanswered questions. When I realized what I was designed to do, my soul was set on fire. Before that moment happened, I, like yourself, was watching as everyone around me seemed to know exactly what and where they were going in life. I felt unfulfilled as well as insignificant to the world and the people around me. I was praying and asking why did I find myself in all these situations. Then He spoke to me almost as clear as day, "Let the mess you live in be your message. Let go, don't be ashamed, and grow." This is when I was awakened to the fact that the two aspects of my life that I struggled with the most were going to be my greatest strengths and no longer my weaknesses. I knew that I could impact people just with my life story and in the meantime the things that I didn't know, I could dedicate myself to loving myself as I would grow. Money and connecting people where my two biggest struggles so from then on, I made it my mission to help other women become empowered to flourish in life. I came up with my own mission statement and searched for avenues to accomplish what I knew I was meant to do.

I believe everyone in life should live with their own mission statement. Businesses and companies have them, so why not me and you. It will help you make quick decisions when you're stuck at a crossroad. When I think of why I do what I do, it fills my spirit with an overwhelming sense of fulfillment and satisfaction. I believe my mission really is empowering women to live to their truest potential in leadership, in love and in life. How I do that is by helping them take away the financial, income and mindset barriers that hold them back and show up myself by being the best personal version of me possible. Since I've dealt with a negative mindset in the past I have seen how a negative attitude can hurt or hinder somebody's ability to move forward into abundance, so I know what it takes to break through its cold walls.

Can you guess what the best part of finding out what my purpose is? I get to give back to the world and create a lasting impact on the lives of thousands just by the actions I take each day. Our greatest purpose is to figure out how we are going to change the world and how we will connect and love other people. If I did not find my purpose, I would not have the incredible relationships I am blessed with today.

Every day I get to fall more and more in love with my career because there are no limits on my income. I control my schedule and work with unbelievable leaders as well as those who I choose to bring into the field. I'm absolutely free to be the creative me I know I was born to be. I'm blessed to travel with my team all around the world and even work alongside my husband when he feels compelled to get involved, which makes me incredibly lucky.

Now honestly, if you told me five years ago that I would be working in finances, I would have laughed hysterically, probably not stopping for five minutes or more due to the fact math was not something I enjoyed growing up. However, I've found a great need in the way people manage their finances today. I get to give people an avenue to express their truest passions when the barriers are broken. Most people do not live their purpose or passion; they do what they have to do, not necessarily what they want to do. I believe life is too short not to do what you love. These days I live my passion by helping others live theirs. Every day I wake up pumped to work with the people I will meet and connect with that day. Each day is such an incredible adventure. I have the opportunity to create bonds that will last a lifetime. Listening and pouring into people's dreams is the most exhilarating part of my day-to-day activities.

When I received my first paycheck, though my mother tried to instill good saving habits in me, when it came time to get control of my finances I did what most sixteen-year-olds do, I blew it on my friends and went shopping for the best clothes and food I could find. See, at that time I still struggled with using my voice and my ability to make friends. I recall thinking at the end of my high school years just how out of control I had become spending money on my friends just to realize that if I dug deeper, I would understand why I had no money despite working two jobs. Money is something emotional, not physical. Most people think that in order to make money, you just work hard. However, it's much more than that. It took time to dive into the limiting beliefs I had about money and what it meant to me. I realized I was always buying affection, particularly when it came to my friends or getting the instant gratification of getting a new piece of clothing to show off in school. I found the deeper reasons why I didn't save money – it was because I didn't feel like I was worthy enough to.

I had to go back and play the tapes in my head from my childhood, watching how my mom worked hard trying to put food on our table. I'd see how the lack of money sometimes controlled her, not that she controlled her money. For all those reasons and more, I made it my sole purpose to give back to those around me. It wasn't until I was able to play those tapes and break those types of barriers in my finances and my mindset that I was able to move forward attracting greater abundance. I learned how to keep it, as well as grow it over and over again. Now I get the privilege to help others to do the same.

I light up when I see the joy in a child's eyes once a couple finally saves enough to take their children to Disney World; when a couple no longer fights about money and gets to buy their first home; or even when I help someone escape a job they dread going to day in and day out. It's not about the money; it's about the freedom I get to give a family. What would your life look like if you had more time or money? Do you have it? Do you feel it? Well, daily that's exactly what my purpose has been. I'm able to help people do just that – dream their best life and then take them by the hand and help them live it.

When we think about our purpose in life, I don't believe it's something that you find – it's something that finds you. I would have never thought that finances were something that I would go into but it just made sense. It wasn't something I choose; it just divinely happened and I'm so happy it did.

I think that God let me struggle to open my eyes so that I can help people understand and love every piece of themselves because if you don't have the income or the resources to help you move forward, you can't truly be free. So, when thinking of your purpose, it may be the thing you least expect it to be. Don't get discouraged if you have not figured it all out yet. You were placed here for a distinct purpose and the reason you will find your way. You have value and are worthy of greatness, abundance, and love. Sometimes thinking about what life looks like if you lived without barriers to your income or time is the place to start. Imagining what you would be doing if you lived in overflow instead of lack or scarcity can answer a lot of questions, pushing you into a world of self-development and love.

Dominique Dunn Malloy

You can read Dominique's next letter on page 139.

My heart beats with Hope and it creates new opportunities for me to prosper and praise my Creator.

~Anita Sechesky

SOUL SISTER LETTER
by Anita Sechesky

Dear Sis; Have you stepped into your divine purpose as yet? You know that feeling that keeps you awake at night. How about those thoughts that you are called for a higher purpose in life? Do you have a special gift and it brings so much joy, healing, or hope to others? Your divine purpose is your ordained God calling. It's all about your expertise and God wants you to use that testimony and make a blessing out of it. Help others; share your story. Maybe you have a gift of baking; then you need to do that thing you want to do. Test it out, take it for a spin by volunteering at the homeless shelter or your church community. You never know where that may lead you. Maybe one day, you will be running your own business and blessing that shelter and all the churches in your area. You get the idea, don't sit on it waiting for something good to show up when it's been inside of you all along. Give yourself the chance to become better. You can do it. You have a gift, and that gift was given to you to use wisely. Do it with intention. Make plans, bring them before the Lord, ask God to bless your plans and to guide you every step of the way. Never do anything without God's blessings; if things go south you decide to blame Him when you never invite your Heavenly Father to oversee anything, to begin with.

Remember, if you are still discovering your divine purpose, you will also know that those same desires were planted in your spirit because God equipped you with those gifts. Although His ways are not our own, God always wants what's best for his children. Stay close to God and many good things will follow you. Although life will not always be easy, you will get through it a lot better than those who don't have our big loving God on their side. Did you know that your life is an example to others? I encourage you, Sis, to continue walking in the anointing of God's covering. His blessings will overtake you and even blow you away. This is the favor of God.

I can't tell you enough how many times I felt so helpless about things in my life, and then God showed up with a solution that shifted my mindset into seeing the bigger picture. I am well aware that God has played a huge role in everything I do. I've learned that despite what others think of me, God still wants to use me for His will to be a blessing to others. It can be in my role as a Registered Nurse, as a Certified Professional Coach and Publisher when I work with my author clients, or just as a regular person. Because God's hands are over my life, I can rest assured that everything I take to Him in prayer, He has already addressed, regardless of what it might be.

Maybe you are still figuring out what your divine purpose is and you haven't had much guidance. I encourage you to find a Bible-believing church that recognizes the gifts of the spirit and the seven-fold ministry. This is where you will be spiritually fed and grow into who you are meant to be.

As for those of you who have carried a vision within your heart for so long, I encourage you to protect that vision by giving it over to God. Ask Him if it is His will for you. Ask him to bless it and wait for the answers because they will come. Ask God to bring in the right people to support and build you up. Be mindful because you will attract snakes who look for what they can get from you. Be careful because you will also meet up with wolves who may try to discourage or scare you. This is when you have something of value. If your enemies are not trying to make things difficult for you, then they see you as one of their own, but if they are troubling you, it's because of what's inside of you and all the plans and purposes that God has declared over your life...the enemy of your soul wants to destroy them.

Your divine purpose is priceless and precious. Remember, if God called you into something, He will give you a unique fingerprint so that you are not like everyone else. You will stand out in the marketplace. You are blessed and highly favored by God. This is the anointing on your life. Embrace it, Sister. There is only one of you and God knows what He was doing and you were created for such a time as this. Walk boldly in faith and let God fight your battles. You will remain blessed and as you take it all to the foot of the cross, allow the blood of Jesus to wash you clean over and over on a daily basis because we must remember that none of us are without sin and to receive the blessings of God, we must remain clean in our spirits. Be filled with Joy as you walk out your divine purpose. This is your God-given destiny. So many Christians sadly miss out on living their divine purpose because they don't have the faith to walk it through. They have allowed the people in their lives to discourage them or they have forgotten that the special gift they have is something that is meant for the greater good. It's not always about your friends and family. Have you thought about that lately? When was the last time you went somewhere and even though you were not meant to be there, you ended up being blessed because of the kindness and generosity of strangers who opened their hearts, homes, and even pocketbooks to bless you unexpectantly? This is what a Divine purpose calling does in someone's life. You become a conduit of abundance. Maybe your services as a business are very focused on customer appreciation so you go out of your way to serve your clients. It doesn't mean that you charge less than what the market value is, nor should you allow others to comprise your value. It means you are an integrity-based business and not like the other service providers across the city who offer similar services but operate in an unethical manner. I've learned as a Christian entrepreneur, that initially I tried to please my customers/clients so much that I literally was giving my publishing services away for free. It was not the wisest thing to do but it was my lack of experience and willingness to please everyone. As time went by, I realized that many other boutique publishers were offering similar services, but charging double, even up to 3x the amount I was charging to unhappy clients. My lesson was to stay true to myself because experience is where real value is placed. I learned the hard way that it's not always easy to please miserable people and that my business is part of my bigger divine purpose which attracts the right people that God brings my way. I will never compromise my gifts anymore. Life lessons will always show what to do and how to correct yourself to protect yourself. Trust the process and allow the Holy Spirit to guide you in all your ways.

I truly believe that we each have a divine purpose and if we feel we don't, then we need to seek God more to hear His voice. What is He saying? What are you called to do? What kind of blessing can you begin to be to those around you? Remember, everyone has a purpose. Everyone has experience. Out of those life lessons, you can see how things unfold for you. Bring everything to the Lord in prayer and don't be discouraged by small beginnings. Every magnificent Oak tree was once a small insignificant acorn. Let yourself grow roots in God's word.

My prayer for you is that you'll discover God's will for your life. May you learn how special you really are. May you be healed of past emotions blocking your progress. May your blessings find you and those who are called to walk alongside you show up! Amen!

Anita Sechesky

You can read Anita's next letter on page 143.

Section Two

Part IV

Self-Love & Development

SOUL SISTER LETTER
by Rose Marie Young

Dear Sis; I was inspired to write you this letter, however, it is also for myself. I will be talking about the importance of having great self-love and transformative self-development. Before I start, let me first ask you this: What do you think self-love and self-development are?

Of course, you know the answer to my question!

In my opinion, it's what each individual says it is. Each person's interpretation is different because each one of us thinks independently. Sometimes we have to experience several things or different changes before we become aware and mindful that we need to develop and change. Growth is a process that's necessary for us to achieve our goals. It's also essential for the renewal of our minds and helps us achieve success whenever we own our true purpose in this world. Self-development is a transformation in which we bring positive and healthy changes to our lives. It is becoming aware and also becoming wiser; it is becoming a better version of our true self. There is a process in improving one's self-love and-self development. It is like building the foundation for a home or any dwelling place we desire to make strong. We become knowledgeable that we need to have self-love and need to develop in every area of our lives. This will help build the foundation for better self-esteem as we evaluate our own self-worth. Growth will help to bring prosperity. New growth will help us to reach new heights in our success. It will definitely take us to the next level of where we are.

My first advice is to always love yourself. Other than God your creator, you should always be considered number one on your prior list. Never depend on others for your happiness. It's in you, my dear sister, to love your very own self. Reach way down and find that love in the inner core of your soul. Be happy even when things don't go your way. With happiness, you will have a much brighter smile.

At times, you should smile and give your face a well-deserved rest. There's a saying "Your face is your beauty." In my opinion, beauty is in the eyes of the beholder. Yes? The point is whenever possible, smile. Take charge of your own happiness.

Eat healthily and drink plenty of water. I find distilled water tastes the best. Add plenty of fruits and vegetables to your everyday diet. Most often the foods that are good for you are usually not very tasty while foods that are considered bad for your health are usually very yumtastic. It's okay to have a small treat once in a while, but for heaven's sake don't get carried away. Eat everything in moderation. Exercise often and be excited about it. Exercise helps to keep your body and mind focused Not only that; it helps prevent you from getting sick. Walking is extremely beneficial. That's my favorite type of exercise. Try walking early in the mornings. I find it is very refreshing and a great way to open your mind. It also releases tension.

Another thing I know that can benefit you is to enjoy the silence of nothingness. Whenever there is silence, there's usually a peaceful calmness. Whenever you need stillness, it's okay to find a quiet spot and just relax. Breathe normally and just take a moment to enjoy the quietness. In moments of calmness, you will be able to hear your thoughts and discern the small whispers of your innermost being speaking to you through all the noisiness of this big world.

To love yourself is to never force love from another person. Learn to enjoy the absence of others and the presence of your own company. Never be stuck in relationships that are toxic. Not only are they bad for your physical health, but these relationships are also bad for your mental and spiritual health too. The effect can be damaging to your very soul. Your bad relationships can not only affect you, but they can affect the people around you as well. Focus on relationships that are healthy and positive. Never compare yourself to others, especially those who honestly think they are much better than you or with those who do not respect you nor appreciate you for the amazing person you are. Love yourself unconditionally. You are beautiful just the way you are. One last thing on relationships. I promised myself I was not going there, but for you my soul sister, I will because I do care. Disassociate yourself completely from those who call you friend, but they do not wish you well. It's not good for your self-love nor is it good for your self-development. Sometimes, you have to let people go in order to find yourself.

As mentioned before, it's okay to be by yourself. Programming yourself to enjoy your own company is very important, even for the sisters that are in loving relationships. Time alone helps you to grow with your self-development. Feed your mind with knowledge. Be open-minded to learn new concepts and find new experiences. If you are broken, remember time heels. Always focus on your dreams and have an abundance mindset. When you are successful, celebrate your achievements but do not put your focus on everything that everyone else has. Focus on your own self and your accomplishments. Enjoy compliments and be proud to be complimented. There's always something to be thankful for so be appreciative and always be thankful. Be creative, for a resourceful mind helps with your self-development and always think positivity about yourself.

The world sometimes can be very harsh and cruel. Rise up for yourself and stand your ground. I know some people will put you down and abuse you, but always see yourself as a winner. Learn to say "No" at times. Always tell the truth and remember that it's important to listen without interrupting when been spoken to. You'll get your turn to speak. This is also part of self-development.

Life can be overwhelming; don't overthink, don't overdo. Overthinking kills your happiness. And – this part is very important – forgiveness without punishment to others is also a part of you loving yourself. Forgiveness is for you, not the other way around. When you forgive, you're mending your soul, you are releasing the bad energy from your spirit, and you're clearing out all negativity. Forgiveness helps you to be the best part of you.

In order to have good self-development management, you will need to take care of your physical body, mind, and your spiritual well-being too. Mentally, most of us are drained by the weight and stress of the world with so many things to worry about. So, definitely, we'll need to take care of our minds. If not, we'll become emotionally drained. Be sure to take a good nap at times. Naps help you to release stress and refresh your body. For our mental health, we can include a rest stimulator to invigorate the brain by doing different activities. Once in a while, to clear our heads, go for a walk or read a book and relax. Always have a positive mindset. Don't stress or worry about things that can make you upset. Give yourself a little treat; maybe go to the hair place or to the nail place. You can even treat yourself by going to the spa. Try some new hobbies like pottery or crocheting. Reward yourself with gifts that will help you to feel better about yourself. Your social health is also important, so associate with people at work or in your neighborhood. Maybe join groups at church, go to the park, or participate in a meet-up group for coffee with friends.

To have a good self-development, you need to connect positively with others. You need to think before you act. For example, if something is not right, don't be the first to criticize or even get into a fight. Drive to have a balanced life at all times. Try to find a purpose in your life and live your life by example. Always practice what is right.

Self-development is also about being morally connected. Spirituality is not all about religion; sometimes it's about your mindset and what you believe to be. It's about being a human; it's about loving yourself and loving others without judgment. We should all be concerned about our well-being and for others. Everything we do has a significant impact on our lives. It is our responsibility to take care of our health. It is important that we all learn to cope and function in our everyday lives. Your ability to function daily in a positive way is extremely important to your overall well-being. It is important to keep an open mind and feel positive about yourself in general. Be comfortable in your own skin and sometimes have fun laughing at yourself. It's good for your soul to avoid being destructive and don't be disrespectful to others. Surround yourself with good people, set realistic goals that you can accomplish, don't be overwhelmed emotionally, and don't attach yourself to materialistic things. Don't attach yourself to negative things or people. Attaching yourself to worldly things can be very self-destructive. If you lose any of the material things, it's like losing a part of yourself and could be very damaging to your mind and your soul. Also associating yourself and becoming vulnerable to negativity is counter-productive for self-development. It can make you become depressed and can even cause you to lose self-control.

Take a break from doing whatever you're involved with because it can become really tiresome. We all need a time-out to take care of ourselves. Most often, we get caught up doing so many chores and activities that we leave ourselves unattended and forget about our self-care. Don't be too anxious about anything; it's okay to relax, become one with yourself, and find a peace that we have inside. If you do get anxious, take a break. It's not worth it to deplete yourself. Express yourself always in a healthy manner – everyone else will respect you because they see that you respect yourself. With your self-development, I encourage you to also add meditation to your overall well-being. It helps you to increase and stimulate your mood to be positive. It helps with depression, self-compassion, and helps you to have healthy emotions. Think of happiness in your practice of kindness and forgiveness. When you are angry, use kind and positive words, which give positive energy. It decreases migraines; it helps you to relax your mind and to feel free; it helps to increase your resilience. So, whenever you feel that you are in need of happiness or you're feeling down or depressed or you just can't find it in your heart to forgive someone, try to relax, take time out and do some meditation.

We exist in a very confusing world, live a very complex life, and yes, life takes its toll on us. It can affect our bodies. Everything we do and everything we attach ourselves to affects our lives to some degree. Loving yourself can be very hard, but it should not be. We try to protect others; however, we need to protect ourselves, our hearts, and our souls from all the negativity that comes with life itself. Love is rather intricate with different feelings and emotions. It's important that you show those good emotions and feelings to yourself as well. Most people forget to love themselves. By loving yourself, you are making room for others to love and I respect you. Stay positive and be comfortable in your own skin. Loving yourself is more important than others loving you. It is my belief that the way you treat yourself and the way you see yourself is how others perceive you to be. When it comes to love, there is no completely true definition or is there is no completely wrong or right way of showing love. Most often we tend to associate love with the search for happiness and we try to find it everywhere and in everyone else, other than within oneself. Love is strongly connected to feelings. It's like having an abundance of different affections caring for one another.

My dear Soul Sister, I hope my letter will help you to feel better about yourself. I know you've always taken care of yourself, but my advice is to always be open-minded. I know there is always room for improvement. You're beautiful and it's all right to love yourself and put yourself first. Everything will improve and you'll have a better and more meaningful way of approaching life. Don't ever give up on yourself no matter what others say. Some will not be kind; people might try to tear you down so take some time and relax. In your mind you know there will be better days although you don't want to even get out of bed or look at the sunshine. Always be true to yourself and know that you are God's child. Know also that He loves you and wants to help you while you're improving yourself. You can stay in your little corner and you can still shine. I think you should just give yourself a break – don't be too hard on yourself. Love yourself no matter what. Don't ever give up but if you ever feel like giving up when times get hard and tough, just look for my letter, read it again, and maybe somewhere it will take you back to a place where you can just relax and enjoy the moment. Know that everything is going to be okay.

Believe in yourself because I believe in you. Love yourself and know that God loves you too. Give yourself permission to think about how you can improve and take care of yourself. Know your true self and walk in your future by faith.

Rose Marie Young

You can read Rose's final letter on page 151.

You can turn your mistakes into opportunities to shift your perception and determine new approaches in life.

~Anita Sechesky

SOUL SISTER LETTER
by Koreen Bennett

Dear Sis; It is interesting how we forget the greatest, most intimate relationship we could have and that is with ourselves. I did not have self-love in my early years (grade school years). I didn't have a good self-image of myself which made me think that I had not developed well. I didn't feel like I truly belonged. You try and find acceptance and love from other people, but how truthful is it if you don't even love yourself? In not liking myself, I was sometimes left with friendships that weren't the best for me. Because I did not like myself, it opened the door for people to treat me in a way that did not help me with my development. I was called names and told that I didn't look beautiful. I remember coming back to Canada after spending a few years in Jamaica with my grandparents. Attending school was a bit of a challenge because I returned speaking a dialect and I had to retrain myself to speak a certain way. I was thin built, flat-chested, hair was in its natural form "not permed or straightened." I did not wear the most fashionable clothing. A young girl thought to tell me how I did not look like her and called me names each time she saw me and laughed about it. I was extremely hurt and felt really bad. I liked her because she was beautifully put together with her hair perm and every strand was in its place. Her clothing was pretty and fit her well. I really wanted to be her friend. I would not say anything to her when she began the name-calling and making fun of my clothing. This went on for a while, and I didn't even realize until later in my adult years that this situation still bothered me.

Lets' go back to my earlier years when it was just me. My mom dressed me in the prettiest dresses and my hair was mostly in ribbons, bobbles, and hair clips. I truly believed I was a princess and in looking at pictures of myself, you could not tell me I was not beautiful or going to do something great with my life. Somewhere between that time and grade school, my thought process changed. I was no longer feeling beautiful but more like the ugly duckling. It seemed I was always surrounded by girls who had cuter figures; the physique I was dying to have. Those were some of the things that I looked at and compared myself to. I used to wonder when I would be like the pretty girls on the television or in the books that I saw. As I went through life, yes, I had friends and I socialized, joined clubs, and had different activities inside and outside of school, but I still had low self-esteem and low self-worth. While the girls on my volleyball team would all be changing in the change room, I would go to the washroom or find an area and quickly change into my uniform. Why? I did not like the way I looked. I did not feel good in my own skin. I wanted so much to be like others, that I was a really "neat girl" and not finding out who I was. I loved writing poems during my pre-teen/teenage years and really treasured reading books. Oh my gosh, I could read forever. I remember winning a couple of prizes for the MS read-a-thon back then. I was a big sister to four other siblings, but I wanted a big sister, even a big brother to defend and teach me. I was searching for likeness, love, and acceptance but what I needed was to love myself and accept me as I was. I needed to do some self-reflecting and assessing the wounds (were they on the surface or some deep cuts?). I would think about how I was going to protect these wounds and allow them to heal (this was the nurse coming out), and just really do some self-care on myself. Many times, that was my prayer request: Can someone be my big sister? I just wanted to not look after anyone for a minute but have some look after me.

As the years passed and I graduated into adulthood, relationships were at times difficult because I was still looking for my self-worth in other people. I thought I would be happy if someone loved me or took notice of me. I still criticized things that I did or did not do right. I didn't realize I was tearing myself down and, in a way, cursing myself. The tongue is a small part of our body, but it can bring such destruction. The tongue can cause mental, emotional, spiritual, and physical harm and damage. I know because I did to myself what others had started. Somewhere along life's journey, I decided that I had to be perfect in my speaking, in my writing, in my dressing, in how I kept my hair. I totally went the opposite of when I was younger. Now everything had to be perfect. Not only did I still not have a great self-image and self-worth, but I went to the other extreme of trying to fix the external part of me by making sure that I looked perfect in the eyes of others and at times, become a bit heartless. To my little sisters, it's okay to be you. It's okay to be unique. God made you that way for a purpose... for His purpose. It's okay to not look like every other sister girl out there. That's what makes you the gem that you are. Not one gem is alike. How BORING if we were all the same shape and color. Every imperfection we think we have is God's unique carving on us. I am asking you to not engage the suicidal thoughts; I am asking you to stop harming yourself; I am letting you know that you don't have to get pregnant and have a baby to bring you that love you are craving and searching for. You don't need to give yourself to every guy who tells you that you're cute and shows you some affection. I want you to know, just like I know now, that I am unique and creative, I am talented, I am successful, I am caring. I am a strong warrior. I am a Legacy Builder and a Generation changer. I have conquered many demons with the help of the Lord.

I realized something as I am writing to you. I did daydream a lot. I also wrote quite a bit, things like poems and my thoughts (yes, I did have a diary). Look at me now: I am not writing a book of poems, but I am writing my story (dreams do come true). I had to learn to be kind to myself and to not criticize and judge everything I did negatively. I believe and know that you will realize the same for yourself. You are the apple of God's eye. You are loved. You are admired. You are FUN, FABULOUS, FANTASTIC, HIGHLY FAVORED!!! I pray for you, my Sister. I pray that you find the greatest love which is God's love. I pray that you find out who you are and whose you are.

> *"But seek first the Kingdom of God, and His righteousness, and all these things shall be added to you."* Matthew 6:33 (**NKJV**)

Father God, I thank You for the beautiful sisters who are reading this book. I pray that You will bless their lives.

Koreen Bennett

You can read Koreen's final letter on page 159.

Chapter Twenty

SOUL SISTER LETTER
by Dominique Dunn Malloy

Dear Sis; When I think of love I think of my mother. When we first came into her life, she would always tell us that she loved us, yet I had to think, "How could somebody who did not birth me love me so much?" This made me wonder exactly what the word "love" meant. I remember as she tucked me in one night, she kissed me on the forehead and said that she loved me. I asked her what the word "love" meant, but she couldn't answer me at that specific moment. The next day she came inside my bedroom, sat on my bed, and patted the spot next to her to come to sit down. That is when she shared with me 1 Corinthians 13 which talks all about what true love actually is. She said that she may not always act as this verse describes love to be, but that's always how love truly is and how she felt about me - she loved me unconditionally, which is why this scripture has resonated with me ever since. When I met my husband, that's how I could see that he was an angel truly sent from heaven because he's a spitting image of 1 Corinthians 13. He taught me a selfless kind of love that I truly had never known until I met him, reminding me a lot of my late mother. He taught me to be patient and kind not just to others but also to myself. Sometimes that's easier said than done especially when your doing it for other people more than for yourself. I'm someone who works hard to be better for my family, my team, and my community. If you're like me and thrive on growing, that can be a challenge some days when you know you can do better. I urge all those who are growing to be patient with yourself and keep taking the steps you need to move forward because for me the only time I was really down on myself was when I felt like I was not making progress and maturing. One of the hardest things to do is to love yourself, understand yourself, as well as being aware of your emotions. It doesn't matter if you've made mistakes in the past or you've failed because it's not those things that make you who you are today. If you realize that each failure can be a learning block on your journey to greater success, it becomes easier to be kinder and more loving to the one you see in the mirror – something we were never taught in school.

This is how I knew I had to make self-love a main priority. In order for others to get better, you must get better. In order to fill the world with your love and truly give back, you first must be filled. You can't influence or inspire another without first being influenced. For most of my career, I worked in management so in that regard, I learned how to give back to my team and those around me. I had to be quick on my feet and be the go-to person in case any challenges arose that day. So, my goal going to work would always be how could I give more value today while making this the best day possible.

The biggest thing you can do to improve someone's life or the situations you find yourself in is to first look at yourself and see how you can change. Do not look towards another's faults but look inside lovingly.

The most valuable commodity that we forget to appreciate, other than the relationships that we build, is our mind that we feed. Just as with a small tree, you must feed it and give it nutrients to grow. You must do this for yourself especially when you have people looking up to you and you consider yourself to be a leader of some sort. You must lead by example. If you're not feeding yourself valuable content, how can you feed another person? You can't.

Our minds play a part in everything. One person will look at a situation and see possibilities whereas another person can look at the same situation and see challenges. This was me in some of my younger years until I read a book that literally changed my life. I could see why every relationship that I perceived as failed in the past didn't work and it taught me how to form unbreakable relationships going forward, which I'm so blessed to now have. But if I didn't search for spiritual nutrients to help me evolve and get better, I would not be in the spot I am today right here before you.

You are the most important person in your life. You cannot support others if you are not okay yourself. Since my goal is to help others, I wouldn't be able to do so properly if I first didn't take the time daily making it my intention to renew my mind and improve. Taking the time to do the small things that really make you happy will make life so much brighter, so sing your favorite song, jump in a bubble bath, and dance around the house when you can. Step out of your comfort zone. Say hi to a stranger and give back when you feel blue. These are all things that will help you enjoy life. You just have to make yourself a priority and not always others.

The wisdom, self-love, and development you invest in will enhance your life because, without them, you're not living, you're disintegrating. They say that when in an airplane, you must first put on your own oxygen mask before you put the one on your child. Focus on loving the most important person in this world – yourself. Concentrate on building your mind and body so you can build your confidence. You are with yourself 24/7, therefore you must become your own cheerleader, your own lover, and your own leader. You sleep and wake up with yourself, so don't tell yourself anything you wouldn't want to say to your daughter or best friend. Then when you're overflowing with pure joy, happiness, and admiration, you can overflow into the world and those around you.

Dominique Dunn Malloy

You can read Dominique's final letter on page 163.

SOUL SISTER LETTER
by Anita Sechesky

Dear Sis; How's life treating you lately? I would love to talk to you about Self-Love and Development. I really think it's something we as believers never talk about enough. In fact, I believe that because of the secular world talking about self-love so often and encouraging others to see themselves as God in every sense, Christians tend to shy away from addressing this topic more often than not, contrary to the very fact that we serve a loving God. Our Heavenly Father is a God of love and it's because of his great love for us that some of us are lucky to even be alive. So, tell me what's not to love about a life we have been blessed with regardless of how undeserving we really are? That's how much we are loved. I have come into the understanding that yes, it can be a very fine line as a Christian. Lest we sin and push God out of the picture. But I boldly claim that I am nothing without Christ, and greater is He that's within me than He that's within the world. Again...why would I not love myself if I am created in God's image and God is living inside of me? As we let go of all the things we see as undesirable about ourselves, we are releasing ourselves from the bondage of judgment of others. As we accept every single thing about ourselves, we automatically start accepting everything about every person we meet in life. Self-love is a reflection of what we are, what's inside of us, and it attracts so much more love into our lives endlessly.

Therefore, I encourage you to join me in these positive affirmations:

YES! I do love myself!

YES! I do love myself!

YES! I do love myself!

YES! I do love and forgive myself!

YES! I do love and forgive myself!

YES! I do love and forgive myself!

YES! I do love and forgive myself so I can create a clean heart and a renewed spirit.

YES! I do love and forgive myself so I can create a clean heart and a renewed spirit.

YES! I do love and forgive myself so I can create a clean heart and a renewed spirit.

YES! I do love and forgive others so I can create a clean heart to encourage myself.

YES! I do love and forgive others so I can create a clean heart to encourage myself.

YES! I do love and forgive others so I can create a clean heart to encourage myself.

YES! I do love, forgive, and encourage myself by the word of God!

YES! I do love, forgive, and encourage myself by the word of God!

YES! I do love, forgive, and encourage myself by the word of God!

YES! I do love and forgive and so I can create a clean heart to encourage myself. YES! I do love, forgive, and encourage myself by God's words to believe that I am a confident, strong, visionary, leader, healer, prayer warrior, and successful woman. I do believe that with God all things are possible for me!

And yes, I often struggle with accepting myself just the way I am. Then I remember what Jesus did for me. I remember that I can do all things and I know that I have a promise that God will never forsake or abandon me. He is as close as the whisper of His name. I love myself because God loves me; God sent his only son to die for me!!! I love myself because I am far from perfect, but God sees me as precious in his eyes. I love myself because I am forgiven of my sins and without God's forgiveness, I could not bear to deal with that emotional garbage being in my daily presence.

I love myself because I know that I can be used by God to bring glory to His name in the way that I treat others with the loving kindness that God has so freely shown me through His son Jesus and other believers. I am free to forgive myself for thinking I wasn't deserving of God's love because the enemy of my soul wants me to believe that I'm not good enough for God's blessings in my life. So, therefore, that enemy wants me to remain stagnant in my personal development and emotional healing which was a result of sinful living or certain things I attracted into my life because of the wrong choices I have made in the past.

As a result, I have now decided to pursue excellence in all my ways. This means that I hold myself accountable for not living up to the excellence that resides within me. I know that I have already experienced the contrast in non-believers, therefore I am understanding that their negative behaviors toward me were a result of their living in their sinful nature. But as a believer, I have the Holy Spirit present within me at all times, so I am consciously aware of my own shortcomings and strive for excellence in the way that I show up in the world. Choosing to love myself is my first step in recognizing my status as a child of God. I have been adopted into a royal priesthood, so there is no going back to my old ways of living. Why would I throw away the keys to the Kingdom of Heaven? I am blessed because of my association and because of that, my integrity has to be kicked up a notch in the ways that I even view the people around me. I appreciate that it's not my place to judge and with that burden of sin removed from my conduct, I can truly love everyone as they are. I see how our choices can affect the results of our lives, so I am mindful of the things I choose to speak; how I do everything changes because things are just not the same anymore. This is what happens when royalty comes to town. We must present ourselves in our Sunday best. We must believe we are worthy to be present. We must understand that there are conditions to be met to be in the presence of royalty. Therefore, we clean ourselves up to be acceptable in our presentation and conduct. We are so blessed.

What a wonderful life we have, as children of God, to be blessed with His unconditional love. We see through all the clouds and know without a shadow of a doubt our God lives, not just yesterday but today and tomorrow ever after. And because He lives triumphantly, we can face anything that life brings our way. This is how our self-development shifts from being totally independent to being fully dependent on God. It might seem backward to some, but in the believer's perspective, we are even more powerful. We are even more successful. We are even more loved and accepted, and we are blessed and highly favored. I am so grateful to God for the freedom we have in Christ to be just what He has called me to be. The world needs healing and as His hands, we can provide that unconditional healing love. We can become examples to one another. We can become the feet that carry the gospel to the nations. We can walk in faith and know that Love covers a multitude of sins and with that knowledge, there is hope for all.

> *"Love is patient, love is kind. It does not envy, it does not boast, it is not proud. It is not rude, it is not self-seeking, it is not easily angered, it keeps no record of wrongs. Love does not delight in evil but rejoices with the truth."* 1 Corinthians 1:13 (NIV)

Anita Sechesky

You can read Anita's final letter on page 167.

Section Two

Part V

Faith Walk

My life is a miracle and I choose to see miracles everywhere around me.

~Anita Sechesky

Chapter Twenty-Two

SOUL SISTER LETTER
by Rose Marie Young

Dear Sis; I'm writing you this letter today to talk about walking in Faith. What brings me to writing to you about Faith is because of my story. I'm telling you because I think it will help inspire, motivate, and encourage you. If it was not for God's good grace, I would not be here telling you this.

My story began when I found myself longingly searching for answers. I questioned why and how this happened. I'm sure by now you must be wondering what I'm talking about. You see my dear sis, I found myself lost and confused from the effects of two major car accidents. It was definitely a miracle from God that I survived. I am so happy and extremely grateful to be alive. I am also very appreciative of the many times that God has blessed and protected me from harm and danger. To Him, I give all the glory and honor.

Because of my survival story, I have decided to be an advocate of endurance and an advocate for God. If you ever have any doubt that He is real, I am a living testimony in evidence, obvious of His true existence.

I was brought up in a Christian family. I literally grew up in the church. Even at a very tender age, I had different experiences in connection with my Heavenly Father. I was an obedient child. However, somewhere during my teen years, I lost my way – confused and distracted by several pulls of this influential world. Over time, I eventually became lost to an unfamiliar world. As I struggled to find my way back, I met so many wolves who wore sheep's clothing. Of course, I had never been warned about such culprits, but even then, in the midst of my needs and my troubles, God held my hands. He has never given up on me no matter how many problems I had. He stood by me through it all. I know that I can always depend on Him. He is available and has been good to me.

I remember many different days when I was at my lowest point. I had no one to call on for help. When I prayed in my dark, cold place, He acknowledged that He heard me. Not only did He hear, but He answered my call for His help. He's an absolutely amazing Good God.

Today I walk and live by Faith. I truly believe that He is in total control of my being. I also believe that I can count on Him and He is always with me in everything I do.

When I was young, I had it all figured out. I focused on exactly what I wanted to do and where I wanted to go. but after I became grown up, things changed. I lost my focus and my vision. I lost the drive I felt when I was just a small child. I became obsessed with friends and even what they had to say. Yes, life was exciting and honestly, it was a lot of fun. Suddenly before I knew it, I was all grown up. By default, my life was turned in another direction. Needless to say, thank God I had my head on straight.

I had to stop and asked him, my Heavenly Father, to forgive me and get my footing back on the right path.

As a grew, I realized that life was nothing like when I was a child. Although some children are faced with great responsibilities, they should not be given. I was blessed to have adults who handled the big responsibilities for me. However, now that I am grown, I had only God to guide me. I'm happy He was there and that He's still here for me. Lucky for me I walked in Faith because I came to an understanding that I cannot depend on my earthly friends.

I was not sure what plans God had for me, but somehow, I was not living the dreams I had planned when I was a kid. I was challenged to try other things and started my life in other directions. I knew not if that was God's plan or if I was given certain opportunities by default. Nevertheless, life went on. He did not forsake me. I was tested many times. But my choices were to fight against the rages of this unfiltered world or give in to it. I choose to fight; to figure it out. Of course, my Heavenly Father had his hand on my shoulders as he also kept his eyes on me. Time and time again, He came to my rescue. Most times, the world was not kind, but God has blessed me. Often my enemies tried to break me down, but I was able to overcome. Not because of my own strength, but because of my faith in an awesome God who has given me my will to survive.

I struggled to stay strong in my Faith, but it became a battle with my enemies each step I took. Again, God was there to hold my hands, defending me every time as only He can.

I had gone through many challenging experiences that I had to overcome before I was able to appreciate all my many blessings. There were as many ups as there were downs. For example, I could not have anticipated being involved in not one, but two multi-vehicle collisions.

My dear Sis, believe me when say I have been through it. The first accident really took its toll on me. It was by God's grace I was able to pull through. Regardless of the pain and the scars, I was determined to recover. However, just as I was in the process of getting back my life on track, I became involved in another life-altering car crash.

So, when I testify that God is good, believe me, that He is. And if you should question me how I know? It's because He's proven it to me in many ways and on many occasions. Most of all, He has and is always with me, not just when I'm in a jam. For that reason, I will never stop glorifying His name and I will never give up on myself no matter what life has challenged me with. Both car accidents did alter my life. I was very angry, afraid, restless, and depressed. I became withdrawn from almost everything and everyone. I was devastated. However, deep down in my soul, I was very thankful to God. He saved my life and has given me another chance.

Both of those accidents changed my life completely. While suffering from pain, anxiety, and a stressful situation, I also had to deal with the fragments of broken trust. With everything that was happening, I was unaware consciously of some of the choices I had made. My confidence was breached and because of that, I became discouraged. I felt ashamed and for a while, I was upset with myself for allowing this awful situation to happen to me. It was through my brokenness that I realized that I need to change my bad habits - I needed a recharge. Most importantly, I also realized that I needed to regain my faith and take back my steps and trust that God guided me to overcome. I stayed optimistic that I would become healed; that I would be someday be excited and happy again. I realized that everything I was going through was valuable lessons. I needed to learn from these lessons and grow. With new growth came a new understanding. I stayed committed to enriching my life by keeping up with all my doctors' appointments, and by focusing on healing and recovery. I also was driven to connect with positive influences and to stay optimistic. Of course, I had to denounce some of my old friends in order to find myself. I also had to give up some of the materials things in order to make room for the blessings that my Heavenly Father prepared for me. I really had to go through some of the experiences of very bad relationships and unhealthy friendships in order to find that only God and God alone could I really depend on. With His guidance, He had helped me through and showed me how to get back on track. He taught me how to use my faith to regain my trust.

Broken trust. My dear Sis, let's talk about this subject. Brokenness is such an important topic to me because at times in the past, I had put my trust in men, and I was very disappointed as they broke my heart. I realized that it's only God you can put your trust in. My dear Sis, I love you, my dear friend. God is not going to break your trust and remember, He will always be there for you and will never disappoint you. Being in those two accidents and surviving them made me realize how special and how important life is. That was definitely a wake-up call that **WOKE ME UP!** It also was the confirmation I needed to reassure myself that my God is real, and I needed to continue my walk as I journey on this world venture with faith.

Also, I want to encourage others to trust in Him and walk in faith as well. When you trust in Him, you need not worry about anything. He will protect you, guide you, provide food and shelter for you. He will defend you, heal you, and bless you. In him, you will feel refreshed, you will feel victorious, and you will feel fulfilled. My God can do that and more. He is an amazingly wonderful ever-giving, ever-loving spiritual God.

I mentioned a bit to you before about broken trust. It is a topic that too often does not get attention, although it's a universal issue. There are so many different aspects of brokenness in this world. People are suffering daily with limited information for them to get help and the tools to heal, inspire, and empower them.

As for me, I had experienced broken trust in relationship breakdowns both in my professional life and my personal life. I experienced broken trust in my financial affairs. It was devastating for me to have my trust in people who did not stay loyal. My financial losses caused me to become skeptical about almost everyone. However, over time I was able to forgive and overcome. I have experienced broken trust in my Wellness. I have experienced so many different forms and categories of brokenness in so many areas. That for me was a wake-up call to help others become empowered. It is my calling to help others who are going through or are dealing with this on a daily basis. My dear Sis, I'm extremely enthusiastic about this subject. The reason being is that it's my greatest passion to help others like myself who are in need of healing. I remembered when I need help. Relationship breakdowns led to broken trust and made me vulnerable to get hurt so deeply on an emotional level to the point that it was crippling. It was devastated and cause me to lose weight and lose trust in even myself. At a certain point, I became angry and very bitter. Because of that brokenness, it caused me to become disconnected from others and over time, from myself. I lost control as it caused me to have very low self-esteem and become emotionally drained. Yeah, financial losses were one of the results and had a very major impact on my life. And not only my life, but my family's life as well. Because of the financial losses, I put my important stuff away, but somehow lost some of them too. I lost my self-value as it was very depressing and at times very embarrassing. I felt ashamed that I allowed myself to be connected with those individuals and then I felt guilty. I was not able to trust for a long time. I really could not believe how it actually affected me emotionally as well.

I came to the realization, after everything began to change, that I needed to give God the benefit of the doubt. I needed to give Him full control. Then I remember a very dear sis I once knew. She believed in God regardless of what she was going through. She had no doubt that God would be there for her. She knew that God loved her. She knew it and felt it in her soul. She was broken beyond her broken pieces, but she was anxious to get her life back on track. God comforted her and guided her until finally, with His love, she was able to mend her brokenness. He was her strong tower. God is able to break down any barrier. She knew in her heart that everything she had lost and everything that was stolen would be one day be given back in abundance because God would restore it all. She also knew that no matter how many mountains she had to climb, she would overcome each one. That's inspirational. Faith is having trust with the commitment that you will overcome.

My dear Sis, I encourage you to pray and read your Bible each and every day. Stay connected with others who share your faith as they will help to encourage you. Some people are truly God's angels in disguise. In this life's journey, you never know who you are going to meet. If one day you should meet any of these angels, even though you may not recognize them, treat him or her with respect and show them love. It is also important for you to know that God's angels may not be the same age as you nor even be the same race. Be accepting of everyone and treat them the same. Remember, God has no preference when He commands the rain to fall. He is good to all. Likewise, when you pray, intervene for everyone, even for those who do not share your own faith or your own vision. God loves the world, meaning He loves us all. Everyone in the world are all his children and should always be treated as such. Be kind and generous to each person. One of our purposes in the world is to share. He has given to each of us a heart conditioned with the willingness to love and to share.

There's nothing like God's grace and God's love. His love is abundant. He has given to us so we can bless others as well. If you are willing to walk in faith, trust that He will walk with you. He promises that He will never leave us nor will He forsake us. You are never alone. There is nothing that He cannot do. When you are weak, He will make you stronger. When you are sad, He will make you happier. When you feel small, He will make you taller.

My dear Sis, I do hope with my letters you have been inspired to take a leap of faith and trust that God will bless you and guide you through whatever you are been challenged with. I also hope that someone day you will be able to write from a place of healing all that you have been through. I also hope with your letters of testimonies, someone else will be encouraged, and I hope my transformation, my enlightenment, and my growth will always empower you.

My Soul Sister, I Love You.

Rose Marie Young

Chapter Twenty-Three

SOUL SISTER LETTER
by Koreen Bennett

Dear Sis; As much as we want to have a positive mindset, life does give us challenges. *"Courage says in the face of adversity I will not quit."* When I feel like I cannot take another step, I hear a little voice say, "Yes you can, just one more, Koreen," and I usually can get two or three more steps in. If you are struggling with disappointment over a relationship, over a dream not yet fulfilled, or you feel it's too late for you to receive God's Promises, I pray that you won't get discouraged by what you see, but know that God is always working on your behalf. His timing is perfect, and He will perform his word, His promises to you. He will show up with such a sovereign surprise for you, my Sister.

I think back to the story in the Bible about Ruth and Naomi. I believe Ruth may be my favorite bible character. She was a widow at a young age, yet she showed courage, loyalty, determination, took risks, and could have gone in a different direction (literally), but she made some difficult decisions and remained with her mother-in-law and God blessed her for that. I have been through some challenges, many ups and downs in my life. When you get the test results that your baby you have been carrying for six months will be disabled, and you're told you will have to quit your nursing career, what do you do? The baby boy you are delivering has the umbilical cord around his neck, he swallowed some meconium, and on top of that, the doctor has to use medical devices to get him out into the world. What do you do? What do you do when your child dies before you, the parent? What do you do? How do you live life? There were many times I wanted to give up and give in, but My God, He sure gave me the strength and the determination to keep going. When Elbert Hubbard came up with the phrase *"When life gives you lemons, make lemonade,"* he knew what he was talking about, right? Well, I think I should have had a few lemonade stands. Life will definitely throw you some curveballs and even send some huge waves your way, but it's how you deal with those curve balls and crashing waves that will show you how strong you are and it might even show you where you need to strengthen up on.

I believe that we are here to do some wonderful things on this earth and the path is not always the smoothest but just keep going forward. I am telling you that God has your back, Girl! Sometimes you don't realize how far you have traveled until you look at your feet and see that God kept your shoes from wearing down. My struggles and stresses were definitely challenges and opportunities that reminded me how strong I really am, encouraged me to keep going, and showed me that I can conquer anything that comes my way. The process is not always pleasant. You never know what will come at you as you go through life's journey: sickness, trauma, life-changing diagnoses, the death of a loved one. Do you feel like you are in a situation you can't change or have a problem you don't know how to solve, maybe in a circumstance you didn't deserve? This might be your journey of faith walk. Maybe you feel cheated out of life and God's promises. I know this might be the hardest thing for you to do, especially when you see no light down that tunnel or the rainbow after that storm. I am saying please trust in God and the process. I've had to learn to trust God in a way that at first, I fought; not going to lie, but I did have to come right back on my knees and call out to Him. He alone knows the reasons and timing. I now recognize that my value and dignity come from Him alone because I belong to God and so do you. God has not forgotten you, believe me. He does have a plan - trust Him and believe in Him. Believe in the One who created you, not only will He show himself to you, He will show up and show out for you, Sister Friend.

I can speak from experience that this Faith Walk has not been the easiest, but it has given me many rewards. I am blessed to have received the seed that was planted by my grandparents many years ago. Because of their faith walk, I am proud to say I am doing my own faith walk. I hope that I can pass on my faith roots onto the next generation. There were times where I had friends call on me to pray with them or pray for them. This gave me the greatest joy because I could leave my situation and help someone else, and it's crazy but in doing that, most times my situation ended being taken care of. God is always on the job.

> *"Be strong and of good courage, do not fear, nor be afraid of them, for the Lord your God, He is the one who goes with you. He will not leave your nor forsake you."* - Deuteronomy 31:6
>
> *"God is your Everlasting Father."* - Isaiah 9:6
>
> *"God is the Lord of Peace."* - 2 Thessalonians 3:16
>
> *"God is your Helper."* - Hebrews 13:6
>
> *"God is your Eternal Life."* - 1 John 5:20
>
> *"God is Love."* - 1 John 4:16

Sister - I hope that you have someone in your life who anchors you when feel like you're crashing along the waves of life.

Sister - I hope that you have that someone who planted a seed of faith love and prosperity into your life.

Sister – I hope that family member or friend is right beside you to talk with you, but more importantly just listening and focusing only on you.

Sister – I hope you have that special person who knows your every secret and you know hers and has it locked in the treasure chest (heart).

Sister – I hope you have that someone who sees you at your best and loves you at your worst.

Sister – I hope you can and will talk openly to God, regardless of where you are in your faith. There is no perfect person, but **I KNOW YOU ARE PERFECT IN GOD'S EYES.** God loves you just as you are and wherever you are at. I ask you to speak to Him like you would a best friend. Actually, He is **YOUR *BEST FRIEND.***

To you, my Sister Friend. With any relationship, where we allow people to come into our hearts, I encourage you to also invite God's only son Jesus into your heart because Jesus loves you. God is your Friend, Healer, Helper, Protector, Provider, and everything that you personally need. I hope that you know that I am praying for you and will pray with you. I ask for God's blessings to rest upon you.

I dedicate this song to you, Sisters. Please take a listen on YouTube: *"Pray for You"* by Raymond To.

"We never understand why we get the road we get to travel on. We might stumble, bump a toe or two, we might fall and remain down for a while, but in getting back up and continuing the journey is truly what matters and shows your true character. The race is not for the swift but keep the momentum going and before you think of being tired, you would have reached your destination."

Koreen Bennett

Chapter Twenty-Four

SOUL SISTER LETTER
by Dominique Dunn Malloy

And this same God who takes care of me will supply all your needs from his glorious riches. Philippians 4:19 (NLT)

Dear Sis; My last and final letter is one I hope you truly connect with because it is probably the most important aspect of all. Just like any relationship, you will have your ups and downs; you'll have times where you have a lot to say or you'll have nothing to say all. Well, that's been my roller coaster walk with my faith. There have been times where I've felt God's presence stronger than ever deep within my soul and known exactly how He's talking to me as well as times that I didn't really hear anything at all, not because He wasn't talking but because I was not actively listening. I was being avoidant, timid, ashamed, and playing small in this world when I knew God had created me for so much more in life.

My faith walk is so important to me because everything in life will tell you that you are not going to make it. If you look physically at what you can see, you won't move forward, but if you look at the visions of your life, to a higher power, you can see all things are possible. You may call it your intuition or your inner voice but call it my loving Father who guides me each day.

Every day, millions of people no longer have made it here to this point in life where right now we both stand and this is nothing but a miracle. I'm sure you've had instances in your own life that you knew if there was just a split-second difference in reaction, you may not be here as well. Each day, people pass away as well as become inflicted with disease and disabilities yet, as one of my great mentors always reminds me, every time we see each other, we made it here to this spot, this day because I am abundantly thankful. But I have to think about why I have made it. Have you ever thought that too? It's not because of our amazing habits or our drop-dead gorgeous good looks, but we've made it here because of something higher and bigger than ourselves.

I've seen how a loving hand of whom I know as my spiritual Father has guided every part of my life to get to where I am today. This is why I know God has put me here for a reason: something greater than myself. I have to give each day the precious respect it deserves, not taking a second for granted because I never know when it may be my last.

Who tells you how much time you have – it's unknown. So, I must believe that if I got up this morning and I'm still breathing, then there's a purpose within my soul. God has a plan for me that is still unfolding; plans to prosper and not to harm me. Every time in life when it got hard, I could fall back on my faith knowing I was never alone. This is why we must constantly move forward. For me, because I believe I wake up each day for a reason, I cannot gamble and play with my time doing something that I do not love with people I do not love. I wouldn't be honoring the life that I'm so grateful to have. I am a vessel for something greater to do its work in me, with me, and through me. That's why I start each day in silence asking for guidance in the ways I must go. I ask my Heavenly Father to put me in front of the people I must know.

If you don't have faith the only thing that would be left is fear and what type of life is that if you're living in a constant state of uneasiness. Fear will never bring out the best in you but faith will. Just think of all those times where faith played a vital part in your life: when you wanted to ask out that cute girl in class; when you wanted to step out and start a business; even when you decided to move to a whole new location. We have billions of decisions to make in one day. How do you choose if you don't have faith? For me, my faith is my compass, my resting rock. It's in my faith that I am never alone; I'm always loved and always embraced.

In the last three years my faith has gotten to the strongest it's ever been as I dive deeper into the Word that gives me strength. If you're open to it, God can speak to you daily in all situations and in all things if you open up your heart to hear. It's something I always love to say: your mind is like a parachute – it only works if it's open. If you are open to the possibilities of what's out there, what's out there will be open to you.

God has always been a constant in my life because I never knew my biological father. I never had an image of what a loving father looked like. The man I grew up with was not the father that I imagined or that I read about in the fairy tales or that my friends would always tell me about. If you are a woman who's had a great father, you are truly blessed but if you are one who may not have had a father growing up, then you can relate to my story because I never had that father figure to fall back on. I never had someone to remind me exactly how to be treated or how a man should treat me until just recently. I accepted who my true Father was. He's the Father who loves all of me and knows me inside and out with all my flaws.

Each failure, each stepping stone in life can push you forward if you look at the perception of things because you can look at it one way or you can look at another way. You will always have two voices in your head: one that tells you to step forward in faith and another that says sink back in fear. Think of what your life would look like u stepped into abundance and development and listened to the inner angel or the inner goddess within yourself, you will start to see that inner voice isn't you but it's your Father. It's the God above and this can lead you into your truest walk and your most loving relationship.

At the end of the day, there will be relationships that come and go, but if you believe there is something higher, you will never be alone. I'll leave you with a verse that says *"He shall give you all you need"* which will ring true if you let it. Right now, if you look in your life, you'll see that you're still here, you're still kicking, and you still have a purpose. God's showing you love right now and giving you all that you need because you are still breathing. Give thanks, enjoy, and let life be your playground, for love will always surround you - I promise, dear Sister, if you open your heart and let it.

Dominique Dunn Malloy

Chapter Twenty-Five

SOUL SISTER LETTER
by Anita Sechesky

Dear Sis; Let's talk about our Faith Walk. If you're like me, you will admit that it's not been an easy journey. This road that we tarry is filled with so many things that test our faith. Then we ask ourselves how we got into situations that we never signed up for! Let me tell you, as a child of God it is not easy. You will grow through your vulnerabilities. You will learn who is real and who is fool's gold. You will shift the way you pray and stand on God's word and promises. Your prayer will become powerful and you will see answers come flooding through. You will experience breakthrough after breakthrough. But it will come with a cost to your comfort zone. You will have to give up that cushy way of handling things and recognize that as a Queen-child of God, the creator of all the heavens and the earth, there is no more room for tolerance. The debt has been paid in full and Jesus' blood has washed your sins away. You are redeemed and You are a free agent to walk in the abundant blessing that your Heavenly Father has said is yours! End of discussion!

We as believers want everything to be just perfect and it can be, but first, we must endure the persecution; we must push past the liars, haters, and mockers who willfully deceive us to our faces. We must cast down vain imaginations that try to set themselves upon us and know that the Victory has been won and the devil is a sore loser. Until that day of redemption, we must proceed with the boldness of being created in the image of Christ our redeemer. We must take up our cross and bear it as we count it all joy because healing is the children's bread. This we can depend on.

We must continue our Faith Walk despite those who fall away. We must encourage others to practice the mindfulness that acknowledges that none of us are perfect but with the daily application of Jesus' precious blood we can confidently wash our sins away. It will bring us closer and closer to that victory of whatever we are facing. It will protect us when we enter into rooms where they may have once spoken badly about us. We must tolerate the ignorance, jealous, and spiteful ways of others without lashing back. We must allow those who sin against us to be placed into God's hands and let Him be our vindicator. We stand on God's word and continually recognize we are so much more than a name, title, and status. We are a blessed child of the highest and living God of Abraham, Isaac, and Jacob. Everything we touch will be blessed to prosper as we walk our faith and talk our faith. We will begin to speak things into existence and yes, we will be able to decree a thing and see it come to pass. Our Faith Walk is powerful once we tap into our source. God is no respecter of persons and what He has done for one He will do for all. So, what's on your heart? Bring it to the foot of the cross. What's troubling you today? Take comfort in knowing that God is already there. Take heart in knowing what troubles you, troubles God and like any parent, God will not tolerate anyone messing with his most precious child. Cry out to God and tell him your woes. Give him the chance to set the record straight. Wait faithfully. Pray without ceasing and don't allow yourself to sin any longer. Set your standards high so you have to leap to appreciate what's waiting for you up there. Keep your heart pure and holy. Walk it out in faith.

Remember, no one said it would be easy, but they did say it will be worth it. Faith without works is dead, meaning you can have all the faith you want but if you speak against your blessings, your prayers will struggle to manifest with the blessings you're expecting. God needs us to be focused on Him as we give Him our worries. Trust Him and watch miracles begin to happen in your life. Pray more for yourself. Pray more for the people in your life, your family, friends, and colleagues. Take the focus off your own situation and lift others up more often. This will create a tidal wave of blessings. As we see what others are facing and selflessly lift them up or come into agreement with them, we are putting tens of thousands of strongholds and wicked thoughts into captivity. We can stand on Psalm 91 and memorize it to become a part of our daily life as we declare God's blessing and protection over ourselves and those we care about. This powerful Psalm, written by King David, covers so many things we still face in this decade. A well-known scripture reads, *"The prayer of a righteous man availeth much."* Well, that's a promise we can stand on to know that we are not wasting our time in prayers. Therefore, we should never cease, until God says so.

I've witnessed so many believers struggle with their identity in Christ because it takes time to build a solid relationship. They go with the premise that God owes them something. They let go of the fact that any relationship worth having must have a commitment from each other. In God's word, He already states his intention towards us many times over. God wants to bless us. God wants to heal us. God wants to prosper us. God wants to restore us and replace what the enemy has stolen from us. And in return, all He asks is for us to love and believe in his one and only son, Jesus, who died for us pitiful, lowly sinners. Yet Jesus was the Prince of Peace. When last have you heard of this ever happening?

I'm not sure if you're facing something that feels uncontrollable and you're feeling like you're backed up against a wall with no way out. Or you may be feeling out of place in a world full of sinners who speak hell and hopelessness into one another's lives. If you're that person, ask yourself WHY?

Faith is a test of our spiritual strength. It causes our weak muscles to be tested and put through things that actually propel us to grow spiritually. Not everyone is trustworthy but eager to get into our business. Pray for discernment so that you can smell the enemy before he dares enter into your presence. This is only a snip of what it means to be a child of God. People will try to break your faith, but it's only you that needs to appreciate the significance of what it all means to be a child of the Most High and loving God.

Why would you choose to step away from being in the center of God's will and attention? Why aren't you ready to release the conceitedness that's been etched on your soul? Understand this, Sister, it appears that there is some deep emotional healing that must be addressed because it's tainting our spirits. It is influencing how others perceive us. It will cause us to feel shame, guilt, anger, and even hate towards those who care more about us. There's nothing wrong with acknowledging your parents to the ends of the earth – how do we acknowledge God our heavenly Father, if we ignore and hold offenses against our earthly father? Forgive, forgive, and forgive once again. Don't ever be shy about choosing the act of forgiveness. As we walk in this direction and standard, we are releasing and setting free the locked-up blessings over our lives. This is a test of faith because if there was no solid or healthy relationship, much less friendship amongst one another, it would still be hard to forgive.

Regardless of your relationship issues, job situations, health status, or financial security, I implore you to walk it out without hesitation. You will get your answers. God will never leave you nor will He forsake you. This powerful journey will make you stronger than you have ever been, as long as you never compromise your position in Christ. Faith is something we must carry within us so that what we believe is manifested quickly and with ease into our lives. Faith holds no records of our wrongs; it is an action word that requires us to act in accordance with confident expectations. It doesn't say to focus on the delay but instead, it is empowered even more by the usage of power phrases such as "without delay" or "immediately." I encourage us all to never forget the power of Faith and how our prayers were answered in the past. It should be enough to make believers out of us all over again.

Anita Sechesky

Section Three

Success happens when you empower your mind and see the greatness within yourself.

—Anita Sechesky

Chapter Twenty-Six

NO GREATER LOVE
by Anita Sechesky

Everyone wants to believe that there is hope in this life despite the circumstances they may be facing. We all want to know that there are answers to the questions that seem impossible and hard to comprehend. Life is not always easy and often times the challenges we walk through can leave a person feeling disempowered and discouraged. The thought of there being some sort of spiritual intervention bringing hope, healing, and a little faith to even believe that things will become better if we only believe and walk in an attitude of gratitude and appreciation is more than many could even imagine; some might even say fictional and far-fetched. There are still those who choose to remain "in the dark" when it comes to stories of God's Heavenly Angels being a part of our everyday lives. We even forget how there have been biblical stories of Angels appearing to mankind long ago to bring warnings, encouragement, and even protection around those they revealed themselves to.

As an individual who has worked in health care for over twenty-five years, I have heard many stories from colleagues and patients about Angels that have been known to bring comfort and inspiration to those who believe. I feel I was very blessed to have my own Angel experience after the loss of my first child. My daughter Jasmine Rose was full-term and born sleeping. It was a difficult time for me, and I had gone through a period where it was next to impossible to even talk about it. I couldn't even pray and asked my husband and mom to pray on my behalf as my heart was filled with so much grief and anxiety. I had completely lost my self-expression to inconsolable tears and heartache because her death was so unexpected. It all unfolded at the time when she was supposed to be swaddled up to come home and live as a little person with her mommy and daddy. Instead, she was born by induction on a busy maternity floor during the height of the Christmas holidays and just days before my birthday. I don't know which part of that experience was worse than the other. Was it seeing the massive knots in her umbilical cord after her birth, and knowing in my heart that I intuitively knew that weeks before? If only someone would have listened to me that something was wrong, Jasmine would have been in my arms that day looking up into my eyes. Or was it the moment when the nurses told me to go for a walk and stretch my legs? And as I walked down that long hallway, it felt as if everyone was reading a sign over my head that I was a childless mommy. They were taking their babies home while I had to go bury mine.

As the weeks went by, the crying changed to fear and then to nightmares. In hindsight, I realize that I entered into a season of Post-Traumatic Stress Disorder. I had no professional support, as my small hometown community did not have a support group in place, although my Physician encouraged me to start a special group for other grieving parents. My hometown had a number of families who had also suffered a similar tragedy. Obviously, I was not ready at that time of my life to take on such a responsibility – I was also walking through that horrific ordeal. My husband dealt with his grief quietly, although he was very supportive of me.

Sometime after our daughter's burial, I started having very disturbing evil dreams that left me terrified and feeling even more helpless and isolated. One particular night I was sitting up in bed reading, and out of the "corner of my eye," I got glimpse of something that completely changed the way I perceived life and that we are living in a world that is multi-dimensional where there are supernatural beings around us, even though we may not see them with our natural eyes. At that moment I witnessed the most astounding sight – right in front of me in full view for that brief second. Although it was not my first supernatural experience, this time it was the opposite that brought comfort and peace around me. I saw the biggest, most beautiful and plushest wings that were swooping down across the bedroom floor, the feathers were of the lushest plumes I have ever seen. I saw arms, the biggest arms with muscles that were formed, flexed, folded across and very developed, and a strong male chest. I saw a Roman skirt with long leather pleats. I saw the leather sandals that were laced up two very strong legs. I saw the sword that was strapped across the chest and hanging to the left side of his body. The blade on the sword was huge and heavy. And then I saw the face of this Angel man. It was the face of a baby, just like a cherub, gentle and yet stern. The look on the face was peaceful and confident. He was on guard at the end of my bedroom, protecting me. My world instantly shifted to understand that I was not alone. God indeed cared for me and He sent his very best to protect and watch over me, despite how fearful I was feeling. I never did have another bad dream again after that night.

There are many times in my life I wondered if there truly was a God, and did he really care about me? I am so far from perfect. I make mistakes all the time. I don't know why Jesus would die for me. I am a nobody. I wasn't born into a wealthy family and haven't made any life-changing discoveries. I don't have a tribe of people around me. I don't think I'm anything special. As I write this chapter, the Easter season is approaching and many people will be off on holidays, celebrating a long weekend with their loved ones and friends. But I really wonder how many people will stop to think of the gentle man called Jesus who was the peaceful storyteller, peacemaker, friend, brother, son. I wonder if they knew His real story and how His life was sacrificed so that one day all the nobodies, somebodies, and those who even consider themselves higher than that, can actually choose where they will spend all of eternity after their time has expired on this earth. I wonder why people scorned him, yet He was so perfect. He never hurt a single hair on anyone. He never lied. He never stole. He never cheated. He never abused anyone. He never took anyone for granted. He never disrespected anyone. He was not a drunk. He was not a drug addict. He was not a lustful man. He was not a fraud. He was not a wife-beater. He was not a delinquent father. He was not a rapist. He was not a child abuser. He was not scandalous. He was not a gossiper. He was not self-seeking. He was not an opportunist. He was not a gambler. He was not a vandal. He was not a murderer. He was not dirty. He was not wasteful. He was not loud and obnoxious. He was not stingy. He was not vengeful. He was not hot-tempered. He was not full of rage. He was not jealous. He was not controlling. He was not a scammer. He was not a liar. He was not spiteful. He did not hurt His parents. He kept His word. He was a good son. He was a good citizen. He was a good friend. He was a good craftsman. He was caring, kind, empathetic, forgiving, thoughtful, trustworthy, humble and meek. He never forgot the poor, the sick, the young, the old, and the destitute.

YET...they hated Him all of a sudden because of their own pride, ego, hate, jealousy, revenge, and most of all, their fear of the omnipotence that came from the heavenly throne of God and the royalty that surrounded His very presence. Jesus shifted the atmosphere because His vibration of purity, love, and peace was so untouchable, lives were changed in His presence. His integrity could not be shaken, beaten, or destroyed, right up to His last breath when He called out, "It is finished!" Where can you find a person that can love you so much that would give up his life? His good life, up until that moment, had been lived with joy and serving His people. He had loyal followers, a family that loved Him, and a career He enjoyed. Yet when called for service, never did He say, "No. I don't know her. I don't know him. Why should I die for them? Look at all the destructive ways they have lived their lives, while I didn't. Why should I die for them?" Instead, He humbly endured the persecution, humility, shame, pain, disgrace, and abuse that should have been for all the sinners who sinned. He who was free of sin took the sin of the whole world on His back, never looking back. What greater love could there be? When His blood hit the face of this earth, the world as humanity in that day and age changed for all of eternity. His blood was shed for all our sins. We who don't deserve, yet He served His life for our redemption, our healing. Our hope is built on nothing more solid, strong, death-defying, disease-curing, life-changing, purifying blood of Jesus. The blood without impurities. The blood that broke the chains off your life.

So today, I ask you, have you found someone who would do that for you? If not, I would like to introduce you to my best friend, Jesus. Your life will never be the same. No counselor, coach, pastor, preacher, priest, apostle, teacher, or leader could ever measure up and one day, they will all look to Him for their salvation as well. I encourage you to find a Bible-believing church that recognizes the seven-fold ministry: Father, Son, and Holy Spirit. It is well. Amen.

Chapter Twenty-Seven

LOVE...IT'S WHAT YOU'RE WAITING FOR
by Anita Sechesky

Let me tell you, one of the most common thoughts I hear about is the fear of commitment when I coach people. Many of my clients have expressed this since everything around them is moving at such a rapid pace, and it seems that relationships are expected to move at the same speed. I have coached so many men and women who are struggling with whether they are ready or not for true love. Many times, we get so busy in our lives with routines and responsibilities that we put aside our longing to be accepted and loved by another person. It doesn't matter who you are and what you do for a living, you have every right to love and be loved. Unfortunately, because of bad experiences and setbacks in life, both genders are in the same boat when it comes to feeling that they are not worthy or good enough to actually find someone who will care about them and accept them just the way they are.

For example, I hear reports from people that after a few dates, the discussion moves to who's moving in with whom. When this decision is made, the dynamics automatically change. People want to be loved and feel secure. Even those who don't move in together feel pressured; somehow believing they have to act in a certain way. Every relationship needs to be taken genuinely without the strain of being too serious and uncomfortable. Therefore, allow yourself the freedom to be just who you are and let yourselves get to know each other instead of pretending to always be someone else. There are so many people who think they have to prove themselves to others and act differently than they normally would around friends and family. You may even be focused on a certain type of person and then expect them to be similar to someone you used to know. How fair is that to the new people you meet in life? It would be no different from starting a job and then being expected to behave and even perform the way a former employee did.

Individuals tend to associate their status with their popularity. If they are single, there's no priority involved in a relationship, which may become neglected anyway and therefore has to fight for its survival. That being said, any personal connection whether it is a marriage, friendship or dating all need to be a central focus of attention in a person's life or it will become stagnant, sickly and slowly die away. I use these terms of comparison to health. Just like we have to keep our bodies nourished and active by giving it the daily attention it needs to be healthy, the longevity of a partnership with someone needs to be addressed as equally as everything else in one's life.

So now if you are ready to have true love in your life, let me ask you this: do you believe it's possible for you? No matter what topic I coach my clients on, if they do not believe in it whether it is a goal or a dream, it can never happen. What you set your intentions and focus on is what you will get out of it, plain and simple. It all begins within you.

At some point, you will have to come to a place of forgiveness and let go of ALL past memories associated with former soul ties, especially if you just started dating or are a newlywed. Yes, I did say ALL! We are complex human beings; we tend to become emotionally attached to people, places and things. If we continue to keep all memories of failed and damaged relationships in our back pocket we will always be remembering, reliving and becoming expectant from those memories. By referencing the things that did not work out in the past, we are missing the things that can potentially work out for us now.

Here is a list of concerns expressed by my clients that can affect a personal relationship with someone:

Fear of being trapped or controlled.

Fear from past abusive (physical, mental, financial) situations.

Fear of being alone causing people to be needy or co-dependent.

Fear of being compared to past partners.

Fear of not measuring up.

Fear of being taken advantage of again.

Fear of having to change for someone.

Fear of commitment based on health issues.

Fear of ridicule from family or friends.

Fear of infidelity.

Fear of not having equal household and financial responsibilities.

Fear of the change in family dynamics.

Lack of motivation.

Low self-esteem.

Given that most of these concerns are fear-based, many of my clients have admitted to me that it really does affect their confidence and self-esteem. When it comes to having a successful love life, any kind of struggle may potentially affect a healthy outcome. Once the fears and limiting beliefs are addressed and dealt with, it becomes easier to attract the attention and satisfaction that they long for. This is where coaching may help individuals learn how to turn many of their negative perspectives into positive ones for a healthy and loving union.

By establishing trust from the initial connection through honesty, you will help to eliminate many fears of the unknown. There should be no apprehension about what the objective of dating really is. For example, do you just want someone to socialize with or are you looking for a life partner? Be upfront and be real. This way, there are no broken hearts and misunderstandings.

So, now that you're ready for love, you know you are not the only one who has had these fears and concerns. You may discover you've got some internal work to do first.

- If not already addressed, start by clearing out your emotional closet, making room for all the positive and life-enhancing things that you want to welcome in.

- Go through the steps of forgiveness, which releases all the memories and emotions attached to past relationships.

This will allow you to be focused on what you really want; something new that will compliment and inspire you to bring out the best in you.

Usually, at this point, my clients are ready to address the things they have been neglecting that make them who they are. For example, is there something they used to do that made them satisfied and connected to themselves? If they have ignored sports, hobbies or interests, there is still a part of them that is unfulfilled. What makes a person so special and unique are the very things that make them happy deep inside.

Now that you have a clear picture of what you really want, you can see that it is possible to even have a goal when it comes to attracting love into your life. When you become focused, your goals become easier to achieve.

Since people cannot be controlled, we have to recognize we can only control and change our own actions and behaviors. For instance, self-esteem is one of the easiest things to change if we can see it that way. Many of my clients quickly understand the connection to first becoming "Love" so that they can attract love into their lives. You see as you go through clearing out your emotional closet, forgiving and releasing old memories both good and bad, your mind becomes void of anything that may have trapped you in the past. You are empowering yourself to become emotionally clear. Now you are ready to receive and give love that is pure and unaffected from anyone or anything else. Congratulations!

The following is an exercise I have used with some of my clients who are ready to meet the "Love" of their lives. Here are some sample questions.

- Write a letter to God explaining in detail what exactly it is that you are looking for in a partner.
- Be specific about their personality; be detailed about their physical traits (How tall is this person? What is their hair color, length, and style?).
- Include their strong points (psychological, intellectual, and physical).
- Talk about your dream life together. Describe what it looks like.

How old is your ideal partner?

- What kind of career does he/she have?
- Do you want children? How many?

- Where do you want to live?

It all begins with you and your choices that will move you in the right direction. If you feel that you would still like to work on some of the things I have discussed above, please feel free to contact me.

Live your life without the limitations of the past or the fear of things that have not yet happened in future relationships. You deserve the best and life wants to give it all to you as well.

Let's work through your limitations now because you really are ready for true love to find you!

What are YOU waiting for?

Chapter Twenty-Eight

SHINING LIKE THE DIAMOND I AM
by Anita Sechesky

When I was a young girl growing up in Northwestern Ontario, Canada, I often daydreamed of what it would be like if I resembled my favorite doll. There she was, just cruising along on the television commercials. All my friends loved her and her entire collection. It was a well-known fact how perfect my little doll was because every girl I knew who owned and played with her was quite excited to have all of her accessories and entourage. I didn't even have blonde hair, but it didn't matter to me. I couldn't believe how much a small plastic doll was loved by all the girls! I just knew it was something big when everyone loves and adores you.

Amazingly, this was one of those major defining moments in my young life because I can honestly say now as I look back, I can see where I had started to apply the art of visualization, as technical as this may seem. Many people don't even realize that they are already applying it in their lives. This type of re-framing and concise perspective is a powerful method that I have used as a professional. I have applied this tool to guide my own clients when they have faced challenges in their lives in order to not be discouraged, to set goals, shift mindsets, and achieve success. Yes, I admit it was a whole different aspect of observing my world when I was a child with limited life experiences to glean from, and yet it was the profound "doll" experience that helped me develop a positive mindset.

Amazingly enough at such an impressionable age, and without the influence of others, I made the decision of what I wanted in my life and I choose to focus on it until I achieved it. This was such a strong mindset which I adapted into my persona that nothing which affected me negatively held me back anymore. I knew what it felt like to not really fit into the right groups and to see all the other popular kids doing their own things together. All that mattered at the time was that I had something to hold onto and pull me through when things weren't so beautiful. Even though I was not the most popular girl in school and my physical comparison was quite opposite to my plastic doll, I trained my mind not to focus on those differences. By accepting this obvious fact, I only saw the beauty in my life. I changed a negative into a positive.

I'm an eternal optimist even though I've experienced situations that were not my greatest moments ever. I know what it feels like when you know people are talking about you as you walk in the room. I know what it feels like when you want to be friends with someone, but you don't know how to fit in or what to say to them. I know what it feels like when things don't go as you would have loved it to, but your friends were too selfish to make you happy. In retrospect, I can see how the energy going to a particular circumstance was the determining factor of this observation. So basically, if I chose to accept that a past experience happened and it did not discourage me from my goals or did not devalue me as a person to the point of causing me to give up on myself, then it did not have to be categorized as my worst experience ever.

I have chosen to process my life events into certain categories. I have adopted this strategy for quite some time, it's been working very effectively, and I can see how far I have come. The place where I am in life right now has been a continual work in progress. It is not a pit stop or even a bus stop. I may not have all the answers to how and what I am going to do about anything. I have been through many life experiences working as a Registered Nurse and the owner of my established publishing company. I will be honest as I tell you there was a time I thought I knew almost everything about human behavior until I learned more about myself. I took the time to understand myself, why I felt the way I did about certain things, and accept that things have happened through no fault of my own. If things were supposed to happen differently, then I could trust that I might or not know about it when the time was right in this lifetime or beyond. In fact, I have come to appreciate the simple fact that if things turn out a certain way, it was for my best interest because if I was to ponder any further, it would just result in causing me further pain and grief. Therefore, I choose not to stress over it more than I have to, and as you can imagine, being an analytic kind of girl, this can indeed be quite a challenging thing to do. Weakness is how we perceive ourselves. Emotions can be our strength or our weakness, it's up to us to determine on which side of the fence do we want to see ourselves over the course of our own lifetime.

One of the greatest lessons I learned was when I understood within my spiritual awakening that I cannot change another human being from being themselves no matter how wrong they may be. It's not my place to even try and change someone's perceptions. I realize that I can guide them through my own knowledge or personal perceptions, but they still ultimately have to choose. We all make choices and the consequences that result depend on our actions and reactions. One way to think about this is how we can beautify the situation into something good. I always look for that glimmer of hope when things seem impossible – that there are no challenges, only opportunities to achieve something better than where I am at the moment.

I have always chosen to have beautiful thoughts to create my beautiful life despite what my reality may actually be. This is where I found my greatest strength by not ever allowing my pain to drown me in sorrow so deep that I could not swim out of it. I choose to always see the surface and look beyond what life was willing to show me. I always believed there was more than what meets the human eyes, and perception is easily altered by intention and emotional intelligence. I'm the type of person that does not like to focus on any negative thing in my life. My conviction for living this way is so strong that I refuse to let my painful experiences keep me down for too long. For example, I recall when I wanted to become a Registered Nurse, I very much disliked algebra, math, anything to do with arithmetic in High School and I never gave it the attention I should have. So when I was faced with having to complete an algebra course in my Health Sciences Program, in which I was required to pass with a mark of 90%, you can only imagine how quickly I made myself fall in LOVE with numbers and arithmetic. That meant algebra became the love of my life. I quickly overcame my strong negative mindset to embrace the fact that "I suddenly loved math." I loved it so much because I wanted to be a Registered Nurse. I recall meeting one of my former High School counselors at a community event. I told him that I was pursuing a career in nursing and his short sarcastic response was to laugh and wish me "Good luck!" I went on to not only to pass the course, but successfully achieved a GPA of 4.0, and I proved to myself and others that nothing is impossible when you choose to believe in yourself and your goals.

For me personally, I have always chosen to be optimistic and not follow the crowd, meaning that if someone didn't like me or something about me, I chose never to become resentful or behave the way they did. Looking back now, I can see that my mom was my voice of reason, encouraging me to let go of any emotional upsets, disappointments, and hurts caused by people I listened to and believed in. So instead of becoming angry and bitter, she encouraged me to choose forgiveness. As frustrating as it was for me as a young woman growing up, I realized that forgiveness was the healthier and sound-minded approach in this life. The latter was never going to give me back the experiences I longed for and lost, or the ones that weren't fair and if I had allowed myself to react from that place of offense or bitterness towards those who lied or mistreated me, it certainly wouldn't have been such a beautiful outcome. Through some of these life events, I learned that people who willfully disrespect and hurt others are more messed up and are so caught up in their own issues that they have no understanding of the negative impact they are making on those around them.

We are all responsible for our attitudes and behaviors. We must choose to cultivate a life of gratitude and love towards others. Each and every action and reaction is setting a tone for what life will give us back. I have learned to personally choose my thoughts and emotions towards others carefully. Having my feelings hurt is not a choice in life, but I have discovered that the negative energy associated with bad experiences and people is not a healthy way of living. It will draw you into a dark and demeaning life where you cannot see the blessings waiting for you because you can only focus on the offense. In doing so, the stress becomes compounded resulting in attracting more of the same nonsense. Why would I want that for myself? Life already has its challenges and because we interact with so many individuals, why focus only on certain people when we have a whole world full of amazing souls waiting to be connected to us.

As for me, shining like a diamond means that I have made a choice to focus on my beautiful thoughts which are the facets of a life well-lived in order to achieve the life I desire. I can now say I have always done so and although life is not perfect, it's how I have chosen to see it. I have walked through many unbelievable events where others have tried to willfully destroy or damage my dreams. Some may have thought they had stolen certain dreams, and even though those dreams may have changed and can never be what they were, I'm sure there's something incredible to learn from those life lessons. I now understand why I never allowed anyone to have that much power and control over my God-given destiny. When you have a dream that guides you into something bigger than yourself, life becomes more than just an opportunity to achieve things. It becomes a deeper spiritual and emotional connection to something greater than who you are.

I strongly believe that all women are connected on a very deep and emotional level. Our lives have value and living in truth requires us to see the priceless beauty in each other and everything around us. The friction that takes place occasionally should never distract us from our higher calling and purpose as we position ourselves for greatness. In fact, they often say that a precious gem must go through a refining process to increase its value, therefore every experience you have walked through has actually made you the beautiful woman you are today. We should always be able to see the beauty and merit of those around us. Truly we are but a reflection of each other, as we were created in a universal sea of love unlimited and in this we will always be.

Excerpted from *Shine Like a Diamond - Compelling Stories of Life's Victories*

Chapter Twenty-Nine

LOVE...IT'S WHAT YOU'RE WAITING FOR
by Anita Sechesky

Inspiration only comes when we remember that nothing is determined by the value others place on us. Inspiration comes from the ones in our lives who could have given up so long ago when others spoke things that could have been our fate.

Inspiration comes from when we see the helpless who have overcome when they had nothing.

Inspiration comes from the wounds that you carry deep inside of you that no one else can see.

Inspiration comes from these wounds that slowly bled for days, months and even years until one day you realized that you and only you could help those wounds to get the help and care they need to truly heal.

Inspiration comes even after losing your first child who had given you dreams to fulfill and plans to make. Inspiration and healing come slowly when you can hear your second baby, a newborn baby boy, cry and coo as you look down into your arms and feel the love of the whole Universe in your grasp that you are a mother again and this time you are feeling the emotions in living color. Inspiration comes when God blesses you again with another beautiful son, your dreams are alive, and they are blessed! God is a good God and as his child, he will find ways to bless you when you least expect it, and in the most amazing and wonderful ways.

Inspiration comes even after you have been told the most hurtful, degrading and spiteful things you would never imagine being told to any other human being, you hang your head down for a brief moment and realize that your will to survive is greater and stronger, and when God and your loved ones are on your side, you have nothing to lose.

Inspiration comes when you have a moment of weakness and cannot take the verbal, mental and damaging abuse from people you respect... thoughts of hopelessness and despair flood your intellect, and you are on the edge, ready to throw it all away once and for all...then all of a sudden you have a vision and see that sweet, innocent, beautiful, precious little face looking at you and realize. Life has only just begun!

Inspiration comes to you when you least expect it...when you realize you have a purpose and no matter what anyone has ever said, done or treated you. You are better than all of that! When you realize that the way people treat one another is only a reflection of what is going on in their world and they are projecting their values and beliefs on you based on their own sad limiting beliefs.

Inspiration comes from the simple pat on the back from a friend or stranger when you have just decided that you cannot do this any longer without confirmation that you're on the right track.

Inspiration comes from the stories of a Grandma who was a widow from the tender age of twenty-eight with eight children, consisting of the eldest being one set of ten-year-old twins and the two youngest were still in diapers, one of whom is your father. Inspiration comes from remembering Grandma only had a grade school education and was given away to live with her in-laws at the precious age of 9 years old. Inspiration comes from hearing how she had no choice but to work after losing my Grandfather, the love of her life.

Inspiration comes in waves when you hear how she had to labor in a rice and cane field with swampy waters and how she was terrified of snakes but had no choice and had to go work. Inspiration comes when I think of how she was offered to be re-married many times and always said, "No" because of how much she loved her children and did not want her family to be separated. Inspiration comes when I think how my Grandma managed to keep and maintain a large piece of land with fruit and vegetable plantations for her children, all by herself.

Inspiration comes to me and fills my heart once more when I remember this conversation with my late sweet Grandma, "Ma, I feel like I don't fit in." "It doesn't matter if you don't fit in...I don't fit in," my Grandma told me on her hospital bed. "Ma, I don't think they really care about me." "It doesn't matter if they don't love you! I love you and Jesus Loves you," my beloved Grandma whispered to me through her pain." Ohhh, how I wished I had crawled into her hospital bed and held her close as she did to me as a child, but I had just finished working and still had on my scrubs and did not want to soil her bed. It was the last time she told me those words before she passed to be reunited with the love of her life my Grandfather who had passed so many years before. I will never forget her love and words of inspiration to me and all of her loved ones over the years.

Inspiration comes from having a mom who was raised by a stepmother, who was abusive and neglectful, and a father who was absent and an alcoholic. Inspiration comes from hearing your own story of how your mom's pregnancy with you was almost terminated so many times and she had to have blood transfusions and was hospitalized to carry you to full term.

Inspiration comes from hearing the story of being a toddler and your parents were told that as a young child with Gastro in South

America. Your chances of survival were next to none, even after being seen by four Paediatricians/Doctors and treated and they had given up informing my parents they should be planning a service. But then understanding that your young parents who loved you so much decided to take turns reading the Bible out loud all night over you while you were sleeping and through their faith and dedication you survived and amazed the doctors.

Inspiration comes and changes everything it can and will change your destiny if you let it! It can be when a stranger believes in you. God and the Universe set it up, and all that was once negative, discouraging, and damaging has now been replaced by all that is positive, encouraging, and beautiful!

There is hope for all that are hopeless! There is uncommon strength for the weak! There is love for the unloved, and there is a place in the heart of those who are compassionate and full of mercy and grace for those who are in need.

Inspiration comes from life all around us. Yes, when I hear the things others have gone through, I realize I have a lot to be "Thankful for" and recognize it's time to give back! Inspiration is all around us. Are you looking? Are you appreciating? Are you grateful?

Inspiration comes from looking past your current situation, seeing what else is out there, how much others need your seeds of hope, and to know and understand their value.

Inspiration is the foundation of a Life without Limitations.

These are bits and pieces of my life story. What is yours?

We all have one. Check yours and see where you were and where you are now. The future never looked brighter! ~

Excerpted from *Living Without Limitations - More Stories to Heal Your World*

Chapter Thirty

GOD'S LOVE IS MY HOPE
by Anita Sechesky

To grasp any kind of Hope in one's life, there must be some kind of loss, fear, negative influence, impending loss, or insecurity in a person's current state of well-being. This is where having a heart of love and gratitude helps to keep you grounded in your quest for Hope. One must also have that divine connection to source, whatever you perceive it to be. The belief that we are all derived from somewhere outside of who we are in our physical state of being can sometimes leave many unanswered questions in a person's mind. For some people, this means a divine connection to our Creator and God of the Universe – that all-knowing, immense presence who sees all and knows all. In these circumstances, there is no question of validity with so many generations aware of this understanding either through faith or ancestral storytelling throughout the years.

Essentially our human spirit searches for a higher influence in which we can transfer our deepest dreams and emotions to a place of ultimate security that is untouchable by all else. It's like we need that soul knowledge and security on some level of spiritual awareness that our divine purpose and destiny are untouchable for those who mean harm in any way possible. I have come into the personal awareness of this very thing through my own observations, whether they were one of the hundreds of previous patients in the nursing homes, hospitals, or general acquaintances I've cared for over the years. It has become obvious to me, based on countless theories and self-help books, that enlightened and heart-centered public figures, motivational speakers, and coaches all discuss how people can be affected by emotional trauma. In doing so, many of them are boldly saying that it's even harmful to personal development and success. What amazes me is despite these resources being so readily available, we often do not give it the acknowledgment and recognition it deserves to be released and healed out of our own lives effectively.

I strongly believe our spiritual physiology is something that we overlook due to the busyness of our lives and therefore it's greatly affected after the most unfortunate of circumstances such as an unexpected health demise or lack of interpersonal strength being developed. If you are constantly working around others who are ungrateful, bitter and reflecting negative attitude and behaviors, you are going to either absorb some of their rotten energy or you will become just like them. We must strive to understand that no matter what we are going through, our lives are still connected so that what we feel, think, or perceive will be precipitated in our actions and attitudes towards everything that affects us.

We must choose to be open-minded and positively develop into the people we want to become – to understand and appreciate others. As we journey inside our hearts and souls, we will discover a desire pulling us into a mindful state of perpetual gratitude, love, safety, and happiness. We might still find ourselves in moments of unpleasant emotions disrupting our inner calmness and security. It's not an easy journey as many will admit because there will be times of confusion and unbalance in our energy. As confident as we appear, we can still become our worst critic and many times the limitations and perceptions that we hold onto are based upon the most unique, disturbing experiences affecting us during times of weakness and vulnerability.

Living in a world filled with instant gratification as the forefront emotion and strong opposition to a world that you may be choosing which is filled with calmness and placidity, you are going to be dealing with moments of frustration and heavy attitudes that leave you feeling nothing but hopeless and insecure. Does it mean you have lost your sense of confidence in what once was or what will be? I am clearly not one to go that route and based on my own personal experiences I can honestly tell you that if you hold onto your strong spiritual sense and sensibility, you will always find some sort of relief come alongside you and spark that hope once more. You will quickly learn it's not about ego at all. It's about realizing that when no one cares, you have the hope to carry on. When no one calls is the time you will find the answers that were never there. When no one helps is also the moment you can see how clearly you were looking in the wrong direction and your sails are now blowing in a new direction in life. Hope will never let you down if you give it the attention it deserves. Hope is as much philosophical as it is emotional. Hope cannot be fake, just as it cannot be mocked. When you find that you have lost all hope is when you will find it in the most unlikely of places. As individuals of reaction and response, our behaviors are based on the things that we are constantly exposed to. They say habits are easily formed by the unconscious and selective process of who we are choosing to be associated with. Many times, if we don't pay attention to these choices, we mirror the behaviors and actions of these very people. It's not always easy to separate ourselves from individuals we have gotten comfortable being around, regardless of the nature of the connection. Because of this, many will continue to stay in damaging relationships, refusing to step outside of their associations. When this happens, we are left in a stagnated growth, emotionally and mentally, all the while life keeps on going. We continue to age and mature as our appearance changes, but our emotional well-being is slowly damaged. Sadly, we allow so many of our life decisions to fall into a familiar pattern of safety. The potential within us is deeply scarred and languishing because we have not allowed ourselves the proper amount of introspective observation to gain peace and solitude with those painful situations. We become limited in our lives. The Hope that should be there to bring in the successes and well-being is constantly overlooked and cannot blossom into what it can become.

For there to be real hope, happiness, and inner healing, we must often choose the act of forgiveness as the positive channel to release all our negative and pent up energy that will dampen and eventually decay our beautiful spirit. By allowing these new and positive thoughts to heal our damaged emotions, we are shifting the energy around us to that of more peace and gratitude. You see, unforgiveness, anger, hate, and especially hopelessness and all its negative behaviors are of low vibration and cannot produce anything good as a result. Hope will never come into its full potential as it was intended to be in our lives, especially if we are still meddling with all those negative and nasty emotions. Too many people are not aware of why they have a false sense of peace and well-being. You see, if one strives for a healthy and confident mindset, all negative attitudes and behaviors must be addressed and determined by what kind of attachments have actually been permitted into one's life. So many times, you will see individuals who attest to having the ultimate achievement we all desire, that of inner harmony and satisfaction, magnified by the power of love, financial security, and social contentment. They want you to believe they've arrived. It's up to you to determine what you see and what they want you to see. Every single person must interact and grow from their interpersonal relationships and daily connections with others. There's just no way you can avoid this human experience unless you completely shut yourself off from interactions and FaceTime with family, friends, neighbors, co-workers, or colleagues. As we become more connected with those outside our inner circle, we then start to examine ourselves differently, as every connection brings its own set of experiences. For example, more setbacks, failures, challenges, disappointments, and opportunities to grow and develop into our best self yet, all of which are prime opportunities to be let down, lose hope and shift our perspectives easily to that of isolation and pain.

Whatever the event, life will always present us with many chances to change our responses; it does not always have to end that way. Our outcomes are solely determined by our reactions, and attitudes play a huge part in our internal temperature gauge. Are we warming up to someone or did we choose to hold something over them? Are we allowing things to slide or are still in a rift with something that happened months or years ago? The choice to be at peace and hold onto hope despite everything is always ours to make.

When we come to understand that being centered is when the heart is at peace, our divine connection to God of our universe becomes confidence that is unwavering and reassures us in times of uncertainty that we can get through just about anything if we believe in ourselves and something bigger than we can conceive. These emotions are so connected and correlate on so many levels, that's why we must come to the full awareness that everything is a choice and our emotional state is also a choice in which we get to choose how we will perceive everything that comes into our fate. We don't get to walk away, ignore, and then complain when everything goes wrong. It's our fault when we fail at getting the expectation of joy or even hope, because once we understand that Hope is a personal choice, we have taken all the power away from those who would want us to believe otherwise, such as those bullies in our classrooms, neighborhoods, or places of employment. Yes, you can even be the owner and boss of your company and have bullies trying to intimidate you and change the temperature of your environment as they feel they can get away with pressure tricks and tactics that make you feel like you are losing your mind and cannot manage your business. I am here to tell you that once you stay grounded and get back on track with your goals and ambitions, you'll find your inspiration will start coming from out of nowhere. People who are in alignment with your beautiful vision will be drawn to you. The energy will shift and those who have no interest will move on. You learned a lesson not to give up on the hope that you created for yourself. Your vision is giving others hope, who have none. Your unique artwork is inspiring others. Your creative music is lifting up so many souls. Your cooking is creating appetites for the most discerning of palates. Don't give up! Don't give in! You've got this! For someone to achieve this state of personal success without the applaud and validation from others, it is choosing to be in simple gratitude and appreciation of oneself. You must understand that life is a story you get to co-create with the people in your life as much as with the universe. Our emotional state is created by our reality, based on our attachment to the outcome, so when seeking an experience in life, we must comprehend that there is a requirement of us to also put effort, and as much hope as possible, into developing the miracle of peace, through mediation, forgiveness, prayer, or acceptance of a situation. We may find ourselves in situations where we cannot get into a meditative or calming state because there's so much happening around us, and we can't achieve the balance and stability we need. It's at these moments that a trained mind will follow the rules of grounding oneself into a place of security. We can do this through visualization, prayer, or positive affirmations. Most people choose to associate miracles and positive outcomes to the understanding that they have deposited a portion of faith, moral thoughts, and optimistic attitudes towards their anticipated outcome. Often, life's painful experiences are the contributing factors causing people to demand within themselves that which makes them invincible. This is also an intricate factor why many people lose hope so quickly without realizing it themselves.

Throughout life's journey, the human spirit perseveres through many difficulties that would have otherwise taken us down had we not had an ounce of peace that prevails. Developing and seeking a life of unconditional hope commences in early childhood and is most often influenced by the content we are exposed to from other human behaviors regardless of who they are and where they fit into our lives. It will impact the very essence of that person who experiences these situations to determine what level of hope they have in their lives and do they want to maintain it regardless of whatever it takes. These experiences may include the loss of a loved one, life-threatening conditions, a devastating diagnosis, traumatic and abusive relationships, family rifts, as well as other moments not fondly recalled. As we choose to remember, what happens may not be directly associated with who you are, but life will always give you experiences aligned to the vibrational energy of those you are closely connected with. You might even be a receiver of the energies from those you are not even associated with any longer. The very nature that you have interacted with someone at any given point vibrationally sets you up for some kind of universal reminder of that person. That's why we must conscientiously strive to develop an intrinsic attitude of unlimited and unconditional hope that permeates from within. We are all responsible beings and emotional intelligence is the reason we have the capacity to gain this ownership of our lives despite our daily challenges.

By recognizing that your life has equal value, just as those you are associated with, allows your higher self to rise and join with others on a more dependable and genuine level. This is a huge deal for those who have suffered from abandonment or offensive and disturbing experiences where they were susceptible enough to allow circumstances to traumatize them so. Although this may have happened unexpectedly, it does not mean it was the victim's fault in any way, shape, or form. It just means that the awareness of the pain has reinforced the individual enough to move them from a victim mindset to self-empowerment and strength to maintain a level of hope and healing involving forgiveness, not only of the individual who inflicted the wrong but an acceptance to forgive one's self for being in the situation, to begin with.

People will carry on doing the same things repetitively, assuming a different result each time, and still not finding the hope and inspiration they are seeking after. Unfortunately, they don't recognize that the resolution is acquainting themselves to a whole new viewpoint that unlocks windows of opportunities, allowing them the ability to heal, evolve, and fluently grow with new and healthier perspectives. I often wonder about those who feel utterly hopeless and how it would impact the lives of those who feel trapped and isolated. Nothing is hopeless if they would only choose to have an abundance mindset and learn to appreciate and love the life they have been blessed with. They must develop a constant method of compassion and love, allowing the peace to be recognized in their connections with others. Letting go of sadness consequential to unforgiveness and pain will permit the stagnant, adverse, and damaging energy and low vibrations to be released from their energetic composition. As they choose to make an effort in their thought processes, emotional intelligence, verbal and emotional triggers, as well as the behavioral feedbacks around them remain positive with higher positive energy from the power of love that envelopes the peaceful aura around and through, creating a simple but significant change in thoughts, actions, and external attitudes. Once we choose to continue attracting more positive and peaceful experiences, it will begin healing our very souls.

Examining my own life, I have also experienced the struggle to hold my peace when I had no control over the outcome based on the actions of the other individual involved. I learned that if there are unsettled events in my life, there will always be some sort of direct disruption and blockage of peaceful blessings and gratitude. This is what permits the renewal of perspectives to create a life shift in future viewpoints and its results.

Hope is a personal journey, but it is conditional on the relations of the people you are associated with. However, it is one of the most powerful things you can do by choosing to step into. May your journey be filled with unlimited hope.

Filter Pain and Find Strength (Bonus Chapter)

How often do you focus on people who have hurt, offended or let you down? Maybe they were not even aware that they hurt or took you for granted because of your loyalty and unconditional support. Is it possible that you gave them the impression that you are an overcomer and nothing could hold you back in life? Meanwhile, you lay hypothetically bleeding your deep emotions all over the place, but they were so inwardly focused on their own life, the people who like them and how much money they could make, they never noticed your pain. One of my most profound discoveries is that sadly, people will continue using you without remorse or regret until they find their next sugar mama or poppa. It doesn't matter what background they come from - when the ego is in control all hell breaks loose in these personality traits. We must always pray and send good thoughts to them so that they will stop using beautiful souls for their own selfish ambitions. That's usually the case if you come willingly into their lives knowing that they need you, so you automatically felt loved, needed and fit in. It's not real, just a facade that is serving one person. Ultimately if you are a person that lifts others up and is always there to catch them when they stumble, they will not recognize your personal value as something that has limits on its withdrawals.

I used to be that kind of person who was always available at any time of the day or night to listen, encourage and give free advice and support. I look back and clearly see the faces of people who generously helped themselves freely to my wisdom and insight, only to watch them go elsewhere after they gleaned everything they could from me. It was a violation of my divine gifting and it was offensive to my very core, but because I was emotionally invested, I could do no harm and would never call them out. It hurt and devastated me many times because my lost trust in those same people affected the way I perceived others. It used to attract more low vibration individuals who had the same intention and sly ambitions to also get as much as possible for FREE from me. It was as if, I had a sign saying "You can't do this to so-and-so but go ahead and do that to her. It's okay, she doesn't understand how smart and valuable her knowledge is as yet." Finally, I put my foot down and stopped that train from going down that track any longer. It was not easy at first, many of them had temper tantrums as any immature and low-level individuals would when they realized they weren't getting any more candy and expensive gifts.

As I consciously allowed myself to inwardly heal the spiritual droughts within my soul, I discovered the beauty of filtering and forgiveness on a whole new level.

Life taught me to search for purpose in the people I now connect with. There are so many incredible moments I could tell of when the emotional insights into other people's lives were automatically revealed to me. I grew in servitude appreciating each person that God brought into my life, career, and business. It was not easy to let go of judgment and fear. In fact, until I understood that my power was in my processing life's significance did I fully see the real beauty that God had given me, which was the ability to be authentically real - not just like a Facebook post but real, real! Embracing real emotions, acceptance of those emotions and the gratitude to see each person completely different than what my physical eyes were showing me.

I encourage you to deliberately filter life and focus on what really matters...you and your loved ones.

Conclusion

Dear Sis; Now that you have read each of these Powerful, Faith-filled, Inspirational Chapters written just for you, my sister co-authors and I trust that you found something that resonated within these pages. It is our collective prayer that you find exactly what you are looking for today.

Please allow me to say an extra special thanks for all the people who have been part of my life and supported my dreams and ambitions, thank you for being the wonderful friends, colleagues, clients and family that you are. I love and appreciate each one of you. Over the years, you have proven who you are, and for that I am grateful.

Once again, I would like to give an unusual appreciation to those who have caused me great pain through the circumstances which resulted in the loss of my daughter, heartaches that have made me lose faith in people whom I thought would never hurt me so badly or betray me, disappointments that showed me how nasty and hurtful others can be, and that I should always turn my eyes upon Jesus and not people. It was because of you; I never gave up. Today, I stand on God's promises that no weapon formed against me shall prosper and every tongue that rises up against me shall be put to shame. Thank you for showing me who you were and the lessons that challenged me to become a better person than I thought I ever could have been. Through all those dark days, I found the strength I never knew I had inside. I cancel every negative word curse spoken over my life and send it back to where it came from sevenfold. I nullify their effects with the blood of Jesus. I forgive you and love you with the love of the Lord, but I do not accept the sin of your curses in Jesus name. Amen.

"I can do all things through Christ who strengthens me."
Philippians 4:13 (NKJV)

I trust that you can see where I'm coming from and appreciate my vision in making your life's journey enhanced with the knowledge that you are never alone, despite what you may be feeling at any given moment. I hope that you will also find the motivation to keep walking in faith that is unwavering. That's why this collection of personal stories, thoughts, and prayers was needed for you to take what applies to you and understand that God's hands are upon your life also. Our unique journeys are not easy, and our burdens are not light but together in spirit we can encourage each other to press on.

I ask you to let go of all your known and unknown limitations my dear sister as you continue to ponder the contents within this book. My co-authors and I have been transparent in bearing our souls to permit you into our individual worlds so you can also identify yourself in Christ and live life to your fullest potential.

Please feel free to reach out and connect with me if something you read within these pages resonated within your spirit. I would like to also encourage you to share this book or gift a copy to someone you know that needs empowerment, healing, and encouragement right now. Us women tend to become complacent in our many roles and forget the value of our salvation. We have the power within us to not only overcome so many things but to bring healing in our midst because of who we are in Christ. It may be as simple as wiping the tears of another sister.

My sister co-authors and I believe our book would be a welcome addition to any church library, ladies support group ministry, prayer groups, Christian women's coffee group, homeless shelter for women and youth, as well as placed in Christian schools where young girls can begin strong discussions about their own life decisions and empowerment as they find their voices in the world.

The value that is within this book is priceless. Just like gold never loses its value, the inspiration poured into these chapters is invaluable and worthy of review and application in one's daily life.

Now, my question to you is, what does your life look like? Are you struggling with keeping your life issues in balance and don't know how to help yourself? Then I encourage you to reach out to those close to you: a church leader, a professional coach or counselor. You can talk to your family doctor if you are having a tough time coping with things. It's not always easy to hold it together whether that involves a company, business, or people and keep things running smoothly while building the life of your dreams. I understand the frustrations, tears, and stress. I want to assist you in making your dreams and goals a reality.

If you would like more support, please speak to someone today instead of suffering another day silently alone. You matter and you deserve to be living the best life possible.

As the Visionary Compiler and main author, I can be available for speaking opportunities. Please contact **LWL PUBLISHING HOUSE** to request Anita Sechesky as your guest speaker or workshop facilitator for your next women's ministry event.

Love, Peace & Abundant Blessings Always,

Anita Sechesky

EMAIL: lwlclienthelp@gmail.com

I Declare...

I am a child of God.

I am blessed and highly favored.

I am healed and walk in perfect health.

I am loved unconditionally.

I am successful in all my ways.

I am wealthy and prosperous.

I am highly favored.

Everything I touch prospers.

My children are blessed.

I am covered by the Blood of Jesus.

I shall not die, but live to declare the works of the Lord.

Amen!

Co-author Portfolio

Rose Marie Young

Rose Young is a Certified Medical Laboratory Technician, Certified Personal Support Worker, and a Certified Cardiology Technologist. She is an aspiring author and an entrepreneur. Rose is the Visionary Compiler of the upcoming anthology to be released in 2020: *Broken Trust - Empowering Stories of Healing for Relationships, Finances & Wellness*. Rose is also a Life Empowerment Coach and currently resides in Ontario, Canada.

Email: rmarie1695@gmail.com

Personal Facebook: Rose Young

Koreen Bennett

Koreen Bennett is a Registered Nurse, Certified Chaplain, Best-Selling Co-author in the book *Living Without Limitations – More Stories to Heal Your World*, and Entrepreneur. Koreen has worked in the health care field for twenty-five years and completed her Chaplaincy course in 2019. Koreen is a wife and mother to two sons (one who is no longer physically here with us). She is also a proud new grandmother to a ten-month-old boy. Presently, Koreen is the Visionary for her upcoming anthology *Carry Me, Father - 30 Stories of Faith's Healing Journey Through Grief*. Her heart's desire is to Inspire, Encourage, and Empower the people she encounters.

Email: koko.bennett@yahoo.ca

Email: kokobennett.kb@gmail.com

Personal Facebook: Koko Bennett

Instagram: b.koreen

Dominique Dunn Malloy

Dominique Dunn Malloy is a newly married wife and works in the Business and Finance field where she is the Division Leader in her Retail Management position for over fifteen years, holds a Mutual Funds Certificate, is licensed through a national Financial Insurance Company, and thrives in management and leadership training. Dominique currently holds all three positions at her local Toastmasters club: President, V.P. of Public Relations, V.P. of Membership and is working towards her NLP Practitioner certification. She is the daughter to two women: one who raised her and the other, whom she grows closer to. Dominique is also a sibling to a devoted sister and a loyal brother, and hopes that by reading this, you can be surrounded with deep love, relationship, and passion in your life.

Email: Dunndo2550@gmail.com

Personal Facebook: Dominique Dunn Malloy

Instagram: dcsmiles25

LinkedIn: Dominique Dunn

Your Legacy Story

Why not write your story and tell the whole world who you are, how amazing you are, and all that you've already lived through? Let me ask you...what's holding you back?

All the times in your life when you walked through situations that you thought you would never endure and yet you found the silver lining, imagine that your life's testimony is the fact that you survived and overcame something that could have truly destroyed all your hopes and dreams. As a registered nurse I have heard so many stories of seniors in their Golden years regretting their life moments they did not document by putting them into a book, just like the many relatives, friends or colleagues you may have known. Those legacy moments were incredible stories of men and women we've personally connected with who overcame struggles, hardships, and events we can't even imagine. Sadly, those beautiful stories of hope and courage were lost when those same individuals left this world. Their stories died with them and their future generations only heard bits and pieces but didn't get the full story. They didn't get a full play-by-play with the emotions, the moments, and the things that determined their strengths to overcome.

What's it going to take you to finally write your story? What about your perspectives? What's helped you to overcome something that you know many people struggle with? Maybe you have a concept about the way that you look at life. Maybe you understand something that other people don't. Maybe life has thrown you some extra special curveballs but yet you figured a way to make a difference, to find your own strength when there was nothing else and no other resources available. You lived it and walked it, so that's why I'm asking you if your story is important. Where would you be today if you didn't have that life experience? One of the greatest blessings I've learned as an author is that the words I write are powerful and even though they may be read by people I'll never meet in my lifetime, the energy of that gratitude, that appreciation, and the thoughts of knowing that it's impacting someone else's life so powerfully and positively, I'm so grateful – and that's how I want you to look at your story, my friend. I want you to recognize that your journey is unique; your journey is incredible; your journey has brought you to where you are and can take you even further than you can imagine. But you've got to take that first step. You've got to write your book. You've got to do it. You've got to stay committed and find a way to make it happen!

Thank you for reading this book, I would love to recommend checking out the first in my new series of annual planners: *2020 WOMAN OF GOD - Inspired Action Success Planner & Journal* available on all Amazon platforms in two versions: full color or a black & white coloring version. This planner will help you to set goals through creating vision boards, mind mapping, and journaling along with inspirational scripture, plus prayer journals & trackers. I strongly believe every woman needs to rise up, set goals, stay organized, and plan to successfully achieve everything she puts her hands to.

Now let's plan a year of friutful harvest.

Amen!

Anita Sechesky

To book a Discovery Session with me, please send an email.

Email: lwlclienthelp@gmail.com

Website: www.lwlpublishinghouse.com

WRITE YOUR BOOK WITH US!

www.lwlpublishinghouse.com

lwlclienthelp@gmail.com

Made in the USA
Monee, IL
23 February 2020